SAAB
TURBO

Osprey AutoHistory

SAAB TURBO

99 and 900 series; 3,4,5 door

GRAHAM ROBSON

Published in 1983 by Osprey Publishing Limited
12–14 Long Acre, London WC2E 9LP
Member company of the George Philip Group

Sole distributors for the USA

Osceola, Wisconsin 54020, USA

British Library Cataloguing in Publication Data

Robson, Graham
    Saab Turbo.—(Autohistory)
    1. Saab automobile
    I. Title   II. Series
    629.2′222   TL215.S2
ISBN 0-85045-502-2

Editor Tim Parker
Associate Michael Sedgwick
Photography Mirco Decet
Design Roger Daniels

Filmset in Great Britain
Printed in Spain
by Grijelmo S. A., Bilbao.

Contents

Above *Saab made their name
famous outside Scandinavia
in international rallying.
This was Erik Carlsson's
Saab 96, being paraded at the
prizegiving of the 1960 RAC
Rally, after winning the
event. Stuart Turner, Ford's
competitions chief, was his co-
driver*
Right *One way not to impress
people—but to prove the
strength of the bodyshell—a
Saab 96 looping-the-loop on
snow*

Introduction

I met my first Saab in 1960. The occasion was the RAC Rally, and Erik Carlsson was driving the car. You don't have to ask if I was impressed. A year later I navigated for Pat Moss, in her Saab, on a British rally, and realized that there was something special about them. In the 1960s I seemed to see a lot of the 'works' competition cars, complete with their 'Made in Trollhättan by Trolls' stickers, and as a press man I got used to being good-humouredly abused by the ebullient Mr Carlsson.

I knew about the top-secret Saab 99 project in 1964, even before I left Standard-Triumph, and drove one of the first examples to reach the UK when it went on sale. These were fine cars, safe cars, and very worthy cars—but no-one would call them exciting.

The Turbo changed all that. It was a brilliant piece of development, which was, and is, one of the most sure-footed, ultra-safe, refined, and enjoyable sports saloons on sale. Before I started to write this little book I borrowed a three-door 900 Turbo to refresh my memory of the layout. I expected to suffer mildly from a sense of *déja vu*, for I have come to drive fast cars of my own in recent years. But it didn't happen. I got out of the car as reluctantly as I had relinquished my seat in a 1978 99 Turbo—and I felt just as safe, and secure, as ever.

In the UK, as in many other countries, the Saab Turbo costs a lot of money, but that doesn't mean the customer is subjected to a rip-off. For what it offers, a Turbo is a great machine, and it suits tens of thousands of people. Read on. This is the story—so far—of its development.

Graham Robson

Chapter 1
Saab's front-wheel-drive heritage

To most motoring enthusiasts, the early years of Saab mean two-stroke fastback saloons, rallying, Erik Carlsson, and that unforgettable noise and smoke. But to a true historian there is more to Saab than that. Certainly the story began in Trollhättan, just an hour's drive up-country from Gothenburg, but cars were not involved at first—the company's original product was aeroplanes. All of which explains why the main Saab car assembly plant is close to an airfield, and why the bare bones of prewar aircraft hangars can still be discerned as part of the much-modernized factory's fabric.

Thank goodness this is not a book which has to concern itself with politics. How, otherwise, could I begin to rationalize the fact that a nation as strictly and obviously neutral as Sweden should need to build military planes for its own Air Force. No matter. In the mid-1930s the Svenska Aeroplan AB (SAAB) had just been formed, had purchased land close to Trollhättan, and was preparing to construct not only an airfield, but a factory where planes could be built. In 1937 the first Saab bomber planes were built, and in 1939 the company expanded by taking over the aircraft interests of the Swedish Railroad Works at Linköping, which was over in eastern Sweden, much closer to the country's capital, Stockholm.

Before the end of the Second World War, in which Sweden had not directly been involved, the design

and administrative headquarters were in Linköping. It became clear that aircraft production would decline rapidly once peace was restored, and the directors began to look around for ways to diversify, and keep their factories, and their labour force, fully occupied.

There appeared to be great opportunities in connection with motor cars. In the 1930s the Swedish private car market had boomed, but there had only been one domestic manufacturer—Volvo. The accent was moving from large American-style machines to more advanced, and much smaller, European cars. In particular, the front-wheel-drive, two-stroke-engined DKW from Germany had been a great success, selling 3568 examples in 1939 alone.

Saab started by building aeroplanes at Trollhättan. This was a late 1930s Saab 17, single-engined dive-bomber and reconnaissance

9

Saab therefore decided that they should start building cars, and before the end of 1945 they had started to develop a new design. Since they had no car-building expertise of their own, and were reluctant to buy in a huge staff of experts who might not produce the right car in the end, Saab made several far reaching decisions. For styling they relied on artist-designer Sixten Sason, who was quite clearly influenced by the way aircraft shapes were developing in the mid-1940s, and for chassis and power train engineering they looked very closely at the DKW which had sold so well in Sweden just before the war. Chief engineer of the project was Gunnar Ljungstrom, who wanted to see aircraft aerodynamics and structural efficiency in the unit-construction bodyshell.

The result of all this design work, which was also

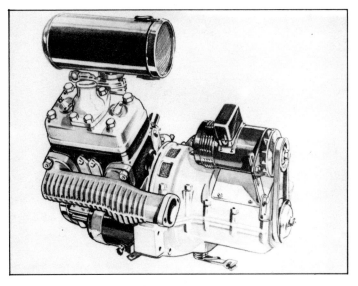

The original Saab 92 car's engine was a two-cylinder two-stroke design. Mated to a gearbox, it was mounted transversely across the car, and drove the front wheels

Left *The simple fascia control layout of the 92B, reminding us that a vee-screen was fitted*

Below *The registration number tells it all—this was the original type of Saab car, the prototype style which became the 92. Aerodynamic shaping came before styling in the late 1940s*

The 93 model of 1957 was a smoother derivative of the 92, and radically different under the skin. It still had front-wheel-drive, but the engine had three cylinders, and was longitudinally mounted

influenced by the work of Gunnar Philipsson, Sweden's DKW and Chrysler concessionaire, was unveiled in June 1947, and the first Saab 92 production cars left the factory in 1949. The original car owed a lot to the DKW, in that it had front-wheel-drive, a transversely mounted twin-cylinder two-stroke engine, a three-speed gearbox (which incorporated a freewheel) and independent front suspension. The car's style was unmistakable, and clearly aerodynamically smooth, featuring a sweeping 'fastback' tail, a V screen, and a smooth nose with faired-in headlamps. The engine's capacity was a mere 764 cc, and the peak power output only 25 bhp. The unladen weight was nearly 1700 lb, so it was not surprising that the 92's maximum speed was only about 62–64 mph.

The new Saab, however, was not only distinctive, but very well built, and it handled very well. Judicious entries in rallies began to build up its reputation for toughness and agility, and its reputation began to spread. The fact that very little of its engineering was actually original was never held against it; Saab, at least, were honest about the origins of the 92.

With every year that passed, Saab sales grew and grew, and with them came the company's urge to build bigger, better, faster and more obviously Saab-designed machines in future. For the moment they were convinced that a two-stroke engine was right for them, and they were already completely convinced that front-wheel-drive combined with a sturdy monocoque bodyshell was an ideal solution for postwar motorists.

By 1955, Saab were ready to announce their next new car which, logically enough, they called the 93. Still using the same basic body style of the 92, which had been modified in detail over the last six years, the 93 had a new front end, new front and rear suspensions using coil springs all round, and—most

A family portrait in more ways than one. The car is the new 96, the aeroplane the Saab double-delta Draken, and the man is Tryggve Holm, managing director of Saab in 1960. It was Holm who did the deal with Leyland-Triumph in 1964, for Triumph to build engines for the new 99 model

Above *Saab's own ghosted view of the definitive 96 saloon shows off the compact front-drive layout, the well-forward driving position, and the generous passenger and stowage accomodation. Note that the underside, apart from the exhaust pipe, was very smooth indeed*

Right *A line-up of front-wheel-drive Saabs, all developments of the original concept. Left to right, as viewed, are the 1950 92 model, a 1956 93, a 1960 96, a 1966 96 V4, and the very last V4 of all, built at the beginning of 1980. The line-up, therefore, spans 30 years*

importantly—a new engine/gearbox layout. The German engineer Hans Müller, no doubt looking at the latest in two-stroke thinking at DKW, produced a three-cylinder engine of 748 cc but placed it longitudinally, not transversely mounted as before; there was also a different three-speed gearbox. It was this engine/gearbox power pack which was to serve Saab so well in the next decade.

20,128 Saab 92s had been built in six years, but no fewer than 53,731 Saab 93s followed between 1955 and 1960. All such achievements, however, were to

Left *Saab's first and only estate car has been the 95, based on the front-end and underpan of the 96 saloon. This, in fact, was the last type 95 V4 built*

be dwarfed by the next new Saab, which would not only spawn an estate car for the very first time at Trollhättan, but which would also appear in various high-performance guises and—for 1967— would be treated to a complete engine transplant into the bargain.

It was this new machine, the Saab 96 (or 95, if the estate car is considered), which really brought Saab to world-wide fame, and to burgeoning sales in many hitherto untried countries. Compared with the 93, the 96 had a brand new passenger cabin, still

Even while developing more and more cars, Saab still found time to build aeroplanes as well, this being the Saab-Fairchild 340

looking unmistakably Saab-like, which is to say that it had a two-door fastback saloon shape with a smooth underside, still with the in-line engine, front-wheel-drive layout, and with splendid road-holding qualities. The engine had been enlarged to 841 cc (and the original power output boosted to 38 bhp), giving a top speed of about 75 mph.

Even though more than half a million Saab 96 saloons, and more than 100,000 Saab 95 estate cars would eventually be built (the last 96 of all not being delivered until early 1980), by the early 1960s it was already becoming apparent that the company would soon require a new engine. The two-stroke unit could not be enlarged any further, was no longer economical enough or (in environmental terms) 'clean' enough, and could certainly not be applied to the new and larger motor car which Saab were already thinking about for the 1970s.

Saab's management therefore made two decisions—one, to go out and buy a proprietary engine for its 95/96 models, was made public in September 1966, but the other, to develop not only a new engine, but a new car as well, had been taken as early as 1964. The new model, eventually named Saab 99, was to have far-reaching consequences for the company's future.

Chapter 2
Project Gudmund and the Triumph connection

At the beginning of the 1960s, Saab were in no hurry to produce a new car. The 96 had only just been put into production, and was a major investment by previous Saab car standards. In addition, it became gradually and unstoppably clear that the new car was going to be larger, heavier, faster and more expensive than the existing 96—and that it would have to be introduced as an additional model, rather than as a direct replacement for the 96.

The first sketches for a new car (it did not take on its '99' sobriquet for some time) were made by Sixten Sason, now with his own independent industrial design business, in 1958, and from 1960 he was assisted by Björn Envall. There was, however, a great deal of sketching before the style even began to approach finalization, and the major question to be settled concerned the engine.

A great deal of nonsense has been written over the years about the engine developed for the 99, even though I have tried to clarify matters on several occasions. It has been said that Saab and the British Ricardo concern designed the engine, and that Triumph eventually took it up for their own use, but this is quite simply not true. The story is much more complicated.

In 1962/63, two projects were beginning to take shape on paper. On the one hand Saab, who still had very little engine-design expertise of their own, were casting round for consultancy assistance. On

Sixten Sason, Saab's gifted stylist, who was responsible for the general lines of Gudmund, which eventually became the 99

Sason and Bjorn Envall were sketching cars on these lines as early as 1958. The resemblance to finalized 99s is obvious

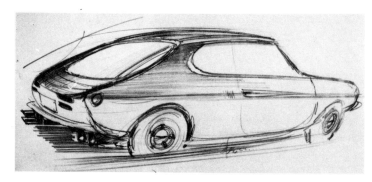

More Gudmund sketches showing emphatically that the car always had the same basic form, even when no more than a gleam in the stylists's eyes

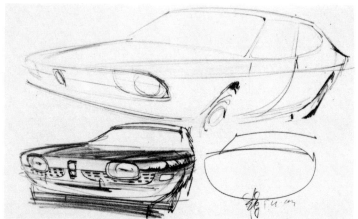

the other, Standard-Triumph (now controlled by Leyland Motors) were beginning to plan an entirely new engine family for the 1970s.

Standard-Triumph's existing range of engines was beginning to look long in the tooth, and technical director Harry Webster instructed one of his senior research colleagues, Lewis Dawtrey, to carry out a world-wide survey, assume that by about 1967 all Standard-Triumph cars would be powered by engines of between 1.3-litres and 2.5-litres, and suggest how a completely new family of engines could cope with this sort of power and displacement spread, with room for 'stretch' and development also built-in.

Dawtrey's survey was masterly. (I have seen the

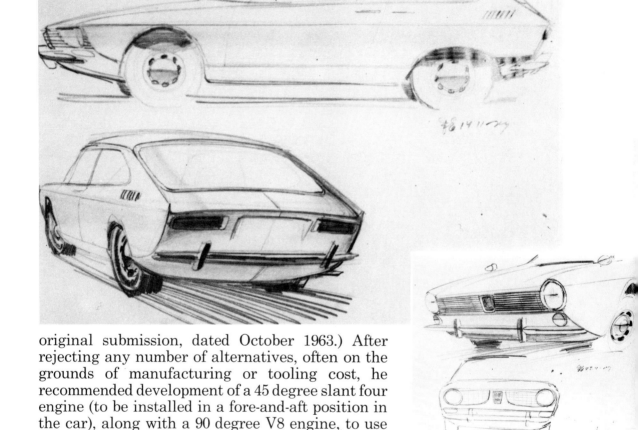

original submission, dated October 1963.) After
rejecting any number of alternatives, often on the
grounds of manufacturing or tooling cost, he
recommended development of a 45 degree slant four
engine (to be installed in a fore-and-aft position in
the car), along with a 90 degree V8 engine, to use
many common components, and to be machined on
the same brand-new transfer tooling. The smallest
'four' could be 1.3 litres, and the largest V8 well over
3.0 litres. Each and every engine would have a light-
alloy cylinder head, and a single overhead camshaft
type of valve gear was recommended.

Standard-Triumph, like many other firms in the
European motor industry, often patronized one of
the two most distinguished British engine design

*More detail Envall sketches
from about 1959 showing
recognizable grille and tail
details*

consultants, Ricardo (the other firm, of course, was Weslake), and during his exhaustive study I am confident that Lewis Dawtrey talked to the West Sussex-based concern.

In the meantime, Saab had also contacted Ricardo who, by the autumn of 1963, had designed prototype 1.3-litre and 1.5-litre four-cylinder engines, the first of which had already been built and bench tested. The original 1300 cc engine was designed for the Saab 96, and installed in an upright position. Meanwhile the 99 car materialized, and the Ricardo engine was modified to fit this larger car—with 1500 cc, and tilted at an angle of 45 degrees in the engine bay. (The very first prototype installed, in fact, had a wedge-spacer between the foot of the block and the gearbox casing.) At the same time the head was converted from uniflow to cross-flow breathing. It always had a single overhead camshaft layout, and was always intended for use with front-wheel drive.

By the time the prototype Saab-Ricardo engines were running, however, the Swedish company had done its sums, and estimated how much investment would be needed to tool up for an entirely new bodyshell, transmission, *and* engine. Frankly, the prospect was daunting, and when Saab's chief executive, Tryggve Holm, got wind of Leyland-Triumph's intentions, he was ready and willing to talk in terms of co-operation.

Holm's first meeting with Lord Stokes, Standard-Triumph's chairman, took place before the end of 1963, and his first visit to see plans for the new Triumph engine took place in January 1964. I was competitions manager at Triumph at the time, my office being situated only yards from the engine development test beds, and I clearly recall the excitement caused by this visit.

The result of these meetings, and subsequent negotiations, was that Saab decided to abandon

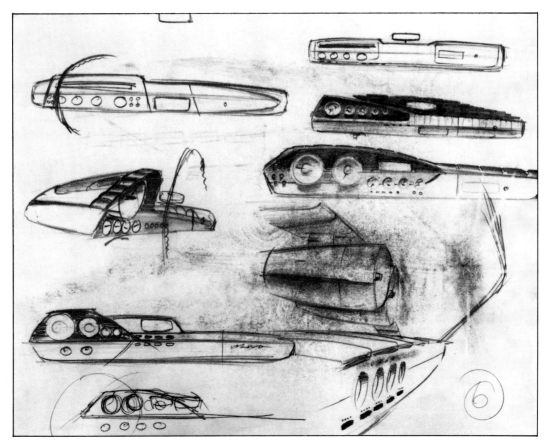

A lot of artistic effort goes into the shaping of a new car. All these were studies for Gudmund, even before the building of a mock-up had begun

their own Ricardo-designed engine, hand over the knowledge gained to Triumph (whose own engine design was not yet complete), and agreed on a common development programme. Triumph (and Ricardo) would build and develop prototype engines, while Triumph would instal production tooling at their Coventry factories. Saab would have first call on the engines, and Holm said that he would need between 30,000 and 40,000 engines a year from 1968.

The new car could now be pushed ahead with great urgency, and on 2 April 1964, only a matter of weeks after Holm had first talked to Lord Stokes, it became not only the 99, but was christened 'Gudmund'. The name, incidentally, is that always applied to 2 April in Sweden—a country where nearly every date in the calendar has a 'name' attached to it—and it was an ideal title for a project which was to stay secret for as long as possible.

I ought, at this stage, to explain where the '99' came from. The Saab '90' series are merely project numbers, issued in strict chronological order, and for years embraced cars and aircraft. The first was the Saab 90 Scandia, a twin-engined airliner originating during the Second World War. The Saab 91 was another plane, this time a basic trainer, while the 92, 93 and 96 were well-known saloon models. Saab 94 was the still-born open sports Sonett with two stroke engine, 95 the estate car version of the 96, and 97 was the series-production Sonett V4 of the 1960s. 98 was the V4-engined Saab 96 (though the name was never adopted for public recognition), and therefore 99 was the next, and logical, number in the sequence.

All the original styling sketches, the small-scale models and the full-size mock-ups, were of two-door saloons, but it became clear at an early stage that the 99 was going to be large enough and prestigious enough for alternative types to be developed. As often happens, Saab wanted to get the 'chassis' and running gear on to the road without the public recognizing anything, so one very early prototype had a 99 underpan and mechanicals clothed by a modified 96 body style which had been widened by

Even in 1963, Bjorn Envall was still working up new ideas for the shape of the 99. Twinned headlamps or rectangular headlamps were worrying him at this session

no less than six inches, by the simple expedient of cutting an existing body down the centre line and welding new metal into place. This grey car, so squat as to be distinctive, was nicknamed Paddan ('Toad' in Swedish), and is now preserved in Saab's own museum. (The first true 99 prototype, incidentally, was badged as a Daihatsu to try to fool inquisitive enthusiasts. . . .)

While the general layout of the 99 was what could be called 'typical Saab', it was entirely new in every way. The bodyshell had a timeless, non-fashionable, style, with a neat grille and rectangular headlamps at the front, but with a more obviously squared-up and extra roomy passenger cabin, but with almost a concave style to the notchback tail. Although there was still a distinct family resemblance to the 96, the shape of the 99 was completely different, and of course the pressed-steel unit-construction body-

At one stage, five different small-scale models were produced to assess various ideas for Gudmund/99. That on the left of the picture was finally chosen for further refinement

*The original type of 99
prototype, of 1966/67, badged
as a Japanese Diahatsu*

Triumph had originally intended to use the slant-four overhead camshaft engine in one of their cars, but because of the Saab contract did not do this until 1972. Here it is seen in the Triumph Dolomite, a conventional front engine/rear drive model

shell was both longer and wider. Compared with the 96, in fact, the 99's wheelbase had been slightly *decreased* (from 98 in. to 97.5 in.), though the overall length was up by seven inches, and the width by 4.5 in.

By Saab standards the 'chassis' was fairly conventional, which is to say that there was independent front suspension by coil springs and wishbones, allied to rack and pinion steering, while at the rear a 'dead' beam axle was located by a pair

of Watts linkages (fore-and-aft aligned), and by a Panhard rod, the suspension actually being by coil springs which bore down on the more massive forward members of the Watts linkages. For the first time on a Saab there were front *and* rear wheel disc brakes.

It was the engine/transmission layout which excited comment, for it was nothing like that of existing Saabs, or of the front-wheel-drive Triumph 1300 which had been developed with the new

The engine/transmission installation in the original Saab 99, as unveiled in 1967. The Triumph-built engine leaned 45 degrees to the right, the clutch and drop gears were at the front of the car, and the gearbox and final drive were underneath the crankshaft

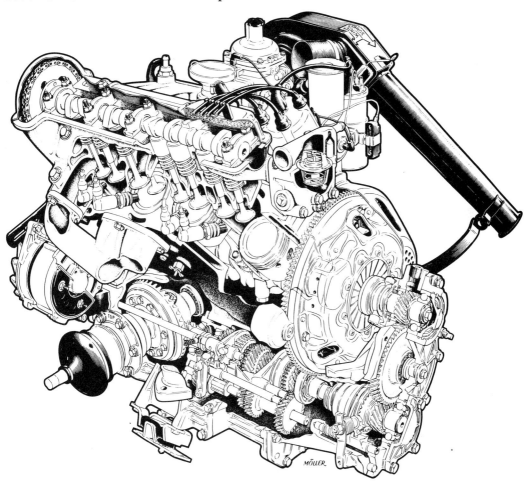

Triumph-Saab engine in mind. In previous Saab 96s, the engine was ahead of the transaxle, while in the Triumph the engine was over the transmission with the clutch and transfer gears at the back, close to the toeboard/firewall. On the Saab, the engine, which was installed at an angle of 45 degrees, leaning towards the right side of the car, was also on top of a brand-new transmission, but in this case the clutch and drop gears were at the front (just behind the radiator), while the four-speed all-synchromesh gearbox was behind the drop gears but ahead of the final drive unit which lived squarely under the centre of the engine itself. The gear lever itself was placed between the front seats (on previous Saabs a steering column change had been standardized), which not only allowed a more direct linkage to be arranged, but also allowed the fitment of a clever ignition key/transmission lock to be located by the lever itself. Naturally, a freewheel was fitted.

Other basic statistics made interesting reading, such as the 61:39 per cent front/rear weight distribution balance, the unladen weight of 2337 lb (much higher than that of the 96), and the very creditable drag coefficient of 0.37, which compared with 0.36 for the Saab 96, and figures usually as high as 0.45 for conventional European cars.

Gudmund, in fact, had grown steadily as design and development progressed, mostly because Saab designers had built in more and more equipment and safety features. Their original Ricardo-designed engines had produced 55 bhp (1.3-litres) and 68 bhp (1.5-litres), while they had intended that the first engine supplies from Leyland-Triumph should be of the new 1.5-litre engines. Almost as soon as the first cars took the road, however, it was clear that the new structure badly needed more power and torque, so for initial production a capacity of 1709 cc was chosen, with a peak power of 80 bhp (net) and peak torque of 95 lb ft; Ricardo-built prototype Triumph engines used single SU or Zenith-Stromberg carburettors, but production 99s were delivered with the Zenith-Stromberg units installed.

While the new car was being developed, and while production tooling was being installed in Britain and Sweden, there were big corporate changes as well. In Britain, Leyland-Triumph absorbed the Rover-Alvis combine, and at the beginning of 1968 they got together with the BMC/BMH group to form British Leyland. In Sweden, Svenska Aeroplan became Saab in 1965, with large new administrative buildings being opened at Linköping, while in 1969 the company

Engine installation view of an early Saab 99, in single Stromberg-carburettor form. Compared with the Triumph, the engine installation is 'back to front', for the camshaft drive is at the passengers' toe-board, and the clutch at the front of the car

*Two ways of testing the 99
included (above) dropping it
on its roof, onto a concrete
floor, to check the strength of
the roof and pillars, and
(right) assessing everything
from sealing against the cold,
and seeing how the engine
started from very cold, in this
—40 degrees C environment*

merged with AB Scania-Vabis (famous for their strong, and well-liked, trucks). Thereafter Saab cars were made by the new Saab-Scania AB group, with the Automotive Division (and engine design) headquarters centred on Södertälje, just south of Stockholm.

The first test drives of true-shape Gudmund prototypes were made in the early months of 1966, and although the new car was not scheduled to go on sale until the autumn of 1968, it was first shown to the press in November 1967. The first 25 pilot-build cars were completed in that year, and sales got under way before the European round of motor shows began in the autumn of 1968.

Once on sale, the Saab 99, in general, was well-received, though the technical press were un-animous in their opinions—it was too heavy, too slow, and not very economical. It was thought to be under-engined—a conclusion with which Saab had privately already come to agree. In the next few years, the story of the Saab 99 was bound up in two main themes of development—on the one hand the evolution of more and yet more versatile body configurations on and around the same basic floor pan, and on the other the production of more and yet more lusty engine derivatives to give the car the performance it so obviously deserved. Saab knew that there was no need to rush any of these developments, as it had always been intended that the 99 family should have a long life—better to 'get it right' in the long run, rather than rush in with changes that might not be completely proven.

The story of body changes is fairly easily told. At first the only 99s on offer were two-door saloons, but from February 1970 this was joined by a four-door version of the same body, which had no increase in overall dimensions, or basic styling. In August 1973, the company unveiled its new three-door Combi coupé (or 'Wagonback', as it was to be called in

North America), which utilized the existing floor pan, front styling, scuttle, screen and front doors. But different new quarter windows and a new sweeping tail and a large lift-up tailgate. This, allied to a folding rear seat arrangement, produced something approaching estate car practicability with the looks of a fastback coupé. With the new and more massive bumpers now needed to keep the North American legislators happy, and with the more sweeping style, the length had increased to 14 ft 10.3 in. (compared with 14 ft 3 in. for the first 99s), and the car continued to put on weight, something like 2550 lb now being normal.

But there was still more to come, for the logical combination of the Combi/Wagonback rear styling and load-carrying arrangement was then made available with the original four passenger doors. Thus, the five-door Combi was revealed in August 1975, and completed the set of four related, but different, variations on the original theme.

It would not be practical to list the engine changes between 1967 and 1974, especially as the added complication of Borg-Warner three-speed automatic transmission (made available from 1970) would make the story even more abstruse. I will merely summarize by saying that in this period we saw 99s fitted with single carburettor or fuel injection induction, produced in 1709 cc, 1854 cc or 1985 cc form, and with power outputs (in European tune) of 80, 87, 88, 95, 100 and 110 bhp (DIN)!

But there is more complication to come. The original 1709 cc engines were all supplied by Triumph, from Coventry, as were the bored-out 1854 cc units. Saab, however, were not at all happy with the general level of quality and reliability they found in the engines supplied from Great Britain, and even before the end of the 1960s they had started making preparations to build their own units. Originally, there might have been thoughts of building engines to the Triumph design, but Saab eventually found it necessary to design their own unit only loosely based on that design.

The whole cylinder block was made longer (there was more space between the cylinder bores—always a benchmark for a major design and investment change), and right from the start the unit was given bore and stroke dimensions of 90×78 mm, and a swept volume of 1985 cc. The stroke was the same as that of the Triumph, but the bore was slightly smaller than the forthcoming 1998 cc Triumph unit, where that dimension was 90.3 mm.

The most important change was to the cylinder head, where the strange angled-bolt method of holding down Triumph cylinder heads was abandoned in favour of conventional vertical bolts, and

Unveiling the 99 to the press, at the preview in the autumn of 1967. Ah yes . . . the days of the mini-skirt!

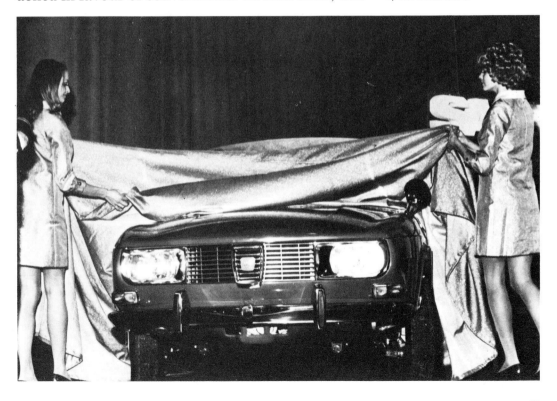

Saab's three-door Combi (called Wagonback in North America), was extremely practical, for the hatchback was also accompanied by a fold-down rear-seat. The Turbo was originally launched in this form

where the new Saab unit was given a line of vertical valves (with a more efficient combustion chamber) rather than the inclined valves and wedge-shape combustion chamber of the Triumph unit. The whole engine was more robust than the Triumph, and looked it, with larger diameter main and big end bearings, and was obviously designed with an eye to the future. It was so designed, however, so as to fit on to the existing front-wheel-drive transmission system which had already built up such a fine reputation for the company.

Saab moved so quickly that they were able to install engine production machinery at Södertälje in time to announce the 2.0-litre version of the Saab 99 in the early months of 1972. The changeover from British-built to Swedish-built engines, however, was only gradual, for Triumph announced the delivery of their 100,000th Saab-bound engine in April, and pointed out that their contract would not expire until July 1972. In the event, 1854 cc Saab 99s were available until mid-1974.

For 1973, however, Saab had a choice of 2.0-litre engined 99s—one type with 95 bhp (DIN) and a

Before the arrival of the Turbo, the most powerful 99 model was this EMS, complete with Saab-built 1985 cc engine, Bosch fuel injection, and 118 bhp (DIN). It was a very neat engine installation, and the styling touches on this two-door saloon are nice too

single Zenith-Stromberg carburettor, the other with a 110 bhp (DIN) rating, and Bosch electronic fuel injection. The problem, however, was that these ratings only applied to Western Europe. Saab, like their Swedish neighbours, Volvo, relied heavily on export business, and were particularly keen to sell in North America. At first, complying with the United States exhaust emission laws had not been too difficult, but legislation imposed at the start of the 1970s meant that all this was about to change. Car makers all over the world came to realize that they could only meet the increasingly tight restrictions by calibrating and de-tuning their existing engines (and making them less economical in the process), and that they could only claw back the lost power and torque by enlarging those engines to compensate for this.

Even before the Suez War of October/November 1973 upset the supply/demand balance of the world's oil business completely, forcing up the price of petrol, and making the need for more economical cars paramount, Saab found themselves in trouble. Even in European tune, the 110 bhp 99 EMS was none too quick, and found difficulty in keeping up with cars like the 2.0-litre BMW 2002s and Alfa Romeo GTVs. When *Autocar* tested an EMS in February 1975, they reported a top speed of 106 mph, a 0–60 mph acceleration time of 10.3 seconds, and an overall fuel consumption of 23.2 mpg. That told one story, but the fact that the Saab was at or near the bottom of all their comparison tables told another.

In North America, where the power of the Saab engine edged inexorably downwards every year, the situation was even more serious. Market analysis suggested that the 99 could only be successful in that continent if it was a safe *and* quick car. Something would have to be done. Should Saab enlarge their own engine, develop an engine transplant, or what?

Chapter 3
The turbo breakthrough
- objective USA

At first, Saab tried all the obvious methods of boosting the performance of their 99 model. The conventional method, of course, would have been to develop an enlarged version of the new Swedish-built 2.0-litre engine. The engineers admit that the engine could be bored out to be about 2.2-litres, but that there was no chance of increasing the stroke due to tight clearances with the transmission, which is directly under the crankshaft. But this, it was thought, would only be playing with the problem—a 10 per cent increase in swept volume

One way to boost the power of the 2.0-litre engine was to fit a 16-valve cylinder head, racing-type fuel injection, and 'tuned' intake trumpets. This was a factory rally car which proved, if nothing else, that too much flexibility was lost

would be worth the same amount in torque. As the 99 moved into higher price brackets in North America, all the indications were that Saab needed a *lot* more power than that.

Perhaps, therefore, the 99 should be treated to a transplant? It was financially impossible for Saab to develop a larger engine of their own (nor was there time to do the job), but because they were still independent of all large groups they could approach several other concerns for supplies. Before the 96 V4 had been finalized, other engines had been studied from Borgward-Hansa, Ford-Germany, Lancia, Triumph, Volvo and VW.

Per Gillbrand was really the 'father' of the turbocharged engine project at Saab, and this is the latest 1983-variety 16-valve engine with which he is posing

Left *In the mid-1970s, the factory competitions department homologated a non-turbocharged 16-valve 2.0-litre engine, with which they used fuel injection, and very 'wild' camshaft timing. The head was different in almost every detail from that being developed in 1983 for production-car usage.*

Below *Scania-Vabis, who joined forces with Saab in the 1960s, were early users of turbocharged truck engines— this massive example dating from 1975*

This was the 99 Turbo engine installation, as previewed to the world's press in August 1976

There was adequate, if not ample, space in the engine bay of the 99, which—when Saab were considering engines of up to 3.0-litres—was probably just as well. Very briefly the company toyed with the idea of extending the front end so that an engine as long as, for instance, a six-cylinder BMW engine could be installed, but discarded it when the investment and handling implications were considered. Several larger engines, including the big alloy Rover V8, were bench tested. Only one actual transplant, however, was physically carried out, and it was really the obvious one to be tried— by a great deal of ingenuity, the engineers managed to fit a Triumph Stag V8 unit into the car!

The Stag V8, of course, was effectively, if not actually, two Saab-Triumph four-cylinder engines set at 90 degrees on a common crankcase, and therefore was no longer than the existing unit. It was, however, considerably more powerful (when fitted to the Stag it was rated at 145 bhp, from 2997 cc), and quite a lot heavier, so there would have been serious cooling and weight problems to be solved if the project had ever become serious. It was

Left *Inside the rotor of the early 1977 turbine. A close-up of the shot below*

Below *This was the original 1977 99 Turbo installation in 'cutaway' form, showing chain drive from crank to gearbox, and the cross-sectional workings of the turbocharger itself*

also known that Triumph were already experiencing reliability problems with their V8 engine; it was just one of several good reasons why the Stag-99 idea never really took root at Saab. Somehow, the 'vibes' were never right.

The third option was to boost the performance of the existing 2.0-litre engine, which basically meant that more fuel/air mixture had to be urged into, and through, the combustion chambers. It was here that Saab's new association with Scania quite fortuitously began to bear fruit. Not many people know that it was Scania, who had been making excellent trucks for many years before they joined forces with Saab in 1969, who were the first vehicle manufacturer in the world to offer exhaust turbocharging, as long ago as 1951, in trucks. Scania, therefore, had a great deal of turbocharging experience, even though this could not directly be applied to the problems of a small (by their standards) private-car unit.

Saab's interest in pressure charging of engines really accelerated when they observed the success of the BMW '2002TiK' in the European Touring Car Championship of 1969, and they, like many other observers, must have been electrified by the performance of the racing Porsches which followed. Although General Motors had been the first to offer a turbocharged road car (in the 1960s, on the basis of a special Corvair), it was the BMW 2002 Turbo of 1973 which was the first to be put on sale by a European manufacturer, and in spite of the fact that this car was launched at almost exactly the worst possible time (just as the 1973 'Energy Crisis' was about to erupt), it caused a great deal of interest.

By this time, in fact, Saab had started developing their own turbocharged engine, for the first prototype units had already been built, and temporarily shelved, *before* the BMW came on to the market. The fact that the BMW was only a partial

This small piece of high-revving kit helps to boost the Saab's power from 118 bhp to 145 bhp without any extra mechanical stress on the engine. Turbochargers are not large, but not simple either, for great precision is needed in their manufacture

success, and had a layout which produced lots of top-end power and precious little low-down torque, actually hindered, rather than encouraged, the development of the Saab system. The fact, however, that Porsche introduced their own splendidly successful turbocharged version of the 911 coupé in the autumn of 1974 was to help enormously.

However, there was still time for the corporate scene to be confused somewhat, for a special 16-valve, twin-overhead-camshaft cylinder head was being developed for competition use, and this was revealed in December 1975, with the magnificent peak output of 220 bhp—or an excellent 110 bhp/litre. It was necessary for 100 such cylinder heads, and associated components, to be built for Group 4 homologation to be achieved, and this was done in 1976. The 'works' competition department used these converted engines for two seasons, and

won several events outright, but all the airy talk about producing a de-tuned version for road use came to nothing, as the rally car had proved to be very 'top-endy', and did not produce the low-speed torque which the engineers were seeking.

The original turbocharged Saab engines had used carburettors, but later units always used Bosch fuel injection. Original units, built as early as 1972, gave trouble, but concentrated work with Garrett on the turbochargers themselves, and on the various controls needed to regulate the boost, led to major improvements, so that by the end of 1974 the engineers were sure that they had achieved a good compromise, and an acceptable design. In particular, the turbocharger itself was quite small, and successful efforts had gone into ensuring good low speed torque, and into eliminating turbo 'lag' as far as possible.

When I asked various Saab engineers if they had ever considered supercharging, rather than turbocharging, I was told that they had, but that they could never achieve the same level of efficiency— 'The only advantage is in quicker response. . . .'

By the spring of 1975, Saab's engineering department was ready to make its presentation to management, and I am privileged to quote from a previously-confidential paper on the subject, which stated, among other things, that 'The 99 EMS is profitable, but it must be fitted with an engine of higher performance with a reasonable added price. The turbocharger would be a solution, as opposed to six-cylinder or vee-8 alternatives, which would be up to 3.0-litres. The advantage is that it could be installed in the *existing* car with minor changes, at only a slight weight increase, with much-improved torque and much the same fuel consumption . . . and it *could* be done within the company.'

(The last phrase of all indicates something that was to be a matter of company pride.)

Opposite page *Turbo on the test-bed. This, in fact, was the latest type of H-engine, (see page 88), which was 11.5 kg/25.4 lb lighter than the original, and more fuel efficient*

Saab's Per Gillbrand, who surely qualifies as 'Father of the Saab Turbo', once said that he always feared that Saab's intentions in turbocharging might be misunderstood, for it was not Saab's idea of what a Supercar should be, but of one which was really two cars in one—and *this* was the secret of the 99 Turbo as eventually put on sale from Sweden.

In the summer of 1976, Saab were at last ready to reveal their intentions to the world, if not to put the car on sale. Four cars were prepared for demonstration to, and trial by, the press, and before the end of the spring of 1977 no fewer than 100 cars were sent out for large-scale testing on the roads of North America, Finland, Germany, Switzerland, and Sweden. Half of the cars were concentrated in North America, the others being put to a variety of uses, on high-speed motorways, in city traffic, or in

99 Turbo at the Frankfurt Show, complete with distinctive cast-alloy road wheels, and Michelin TRX tyres. Somehow it didn't look as sinister, and as muscular, if it wasn't painted black. . .

the mountains of Western Europe. By the end of May 1977, the production specification had been frozen.

Saab's turbocharging philosophy was that it gave them a way to 'reduce exhaust energy losses, and temporarily increase engine performance. This can be done without increasing the vehicle's fuel consumption, because 85 per cent of the time we will only be running on light load. With the Type BZ engine [Saab's internal code for the new 2.0-litre four-cylinder unit] we have 45/50 per cent more torque than current normally aspirated engines. . . . A corresponding increase in torque with normally aspirated engines would demand at least a six-cylinder engine of 3.0-litres, a 40/45 kg (88/100 lb) increase in engine weight, and a 20/25 per cent increase in fuel consumption. Such an engine

requires a larger engine compartment, a larger car, greater weight, and thus we would be in a vicious circle.'

Once again I am grateful to be allowed to quote from another of Per Gillbrand's submissions to his management colleagues in April 1975.

The most remarkable thing which Saab discovered for themselves—and it was a fact confirmed by independent sources in due course—was that the turbocharged engine was only used *as such* in a Saab installation for about 15 per cent of the time the car was in use. By this Saab meant that if they measured the number of times, and the duration, in which the pressure in the inlet manifolds was actually over that of the atmosphere, this only happened for 15 per cent of the total driving period.

There was a great deal of debate about the specification of the Saab Turbo engine, and the philosophy behind it, in the year which elapsed before the production car was put on the market. In many ways this suited Saab very well indeed, for they could be sure that the technical press would also have time to look carefully at the rest of the car, when it was announced at the Frankfurt Motor Show in September 1977.

The new car, which went on sale almost immediately, was known as the 99 Turbo, an obvious and logical title. It is often forgotten, incidentally, that the Saab car division of Saab-Scania had just gone through a rather traumatic year. There had been a tentative proposal for Saab-Scania to merge with the Volvo group, in the hope that longer production runs, and a more logical all-Swedish approach to future marketing would bring benefits. In the long run this would inevitably have led to commonized new models from Saab and Volvo, which was never going to be easy, as Saab was wedded to front-wheel-drive and Volvo to rear-wheel-drive; in addition the merits of merging the

two truck divisions, which made very similar heavy products, were not as obvious as hoped. The merger was speedily abandoned, and things returned to normal before the end of the year.

The turbocharged engine of the production car was helped along by the Garrett AiResearch T3 instrument, the first of a new generation of small units, and at first the Saab designed wastegate (to limit boost pressures) was operated by sensing exhaust manifold pressure. Saab's philosophy had always been to make the turbocharging start to

In the early days, it was almost de rigeur *to have a 99 Turbo in black. Not quite the 'baddy' image, nor the* Darth Vader, *but certainly a most impressive chunk of car. 'Turbo' was on the grille, the flanks and on the tail. Overtaken motorists had no excuse for not knowing what had just flashed past!*

A 99 Turbo cornered very tenaciously indeed, helped along by the radial ply tyres and the front-wheel-drive. The front spoiler, under the bumper, was effective, and not merely for show

work from relatively low engine speeds, and the torque curves they published showed that this had indeed been achieved, for peak torque occurred at the very moderate speed of 3000 rpm. The design of wastegate was an important reason for this achievement. This gives the lie to suggestions that early experience had been gained with turbocharged V4 engines in 'works' 96 rallycross competition cars, for these were definitely only intended for peak revs work, and the turbocharger was a large instrument quite incapable of providing low-speed torque! The first of these special rallycross cars, incidentally, appeared in 1976.

Turbocharging can give rise to a nightmare of pipework under a compactly laid out bonnet, but

the Saab Turbo itself was not too daunting for an owner to contemplate. The engine was laid over towards the right side of the car, at 45 degrees, as with every other type of Saab 99. This allowed the main inlet manifolding and the fuel supply details of the Bosch injection system to be laid out alongside it. The turbocharger itself was ahead of the engine, and just to the right (or exhaust side) of it, tucked in behind the cooling radiator, so that the hot exhaust gases needed to turn the turbine could easily be led into it, while the pressurized air to the inlet manifold could be taken across the front of the engine towards the inlet manifold itself. The turbocharger itself could rev up to at least 100,000 rpm when working hard—even at an engine speed

At first, all 99 Turbos were built with three-door Combi/Wagonback bodies. The spoiler at the base of the rear window was positioned after a lot of wind tunnel development

of 3500 rpm (just over the torque peak) the turbo speed was 50,000 rpm.

Naturally, the boost to power and torque outputs was considerable. For comparison, here are the peak ratings for all Saab's 1978-model engines, in Western European tune:

Model	Peak power rpm	Peak torque rpm
2.0-litre, single carb.	100 @ 5200	119 @ 3500
2.0-litre, fuel injection	118 @ 5500	123 @ 3700
2.0-litre, fuel injection, plus turbocharger	145 @ 5000	174 @ 3000

The basic engine had had to be changed very little to make it into a turbocharged unit, for the same cylinder block, heads, crankshaft, bearings and connecting rods were all carried over unaltered. Because of the higher power available, and the much higher combustion chamber temperatures experienced, the un-blown compression was reduced from 9.2 to 7.2:1 by using different pistons, while sodium-filled exhaust valves were specified. On these early engines the camshaft profile itself was altered, while the water radiator was enlarged and an engine oil cooler was specified for the first time. The maximum turbo boost was set at 0.7 Bar (10.1 psi), and there was an rpm limiter, and an excess boost monitor to make sure the engine did not over pressure itself if the wastegate should somehow not work properly.

The boost due to turbocharging did not look so startling on the 'home market' cars, but on cars destined for the United States it was more obvious, both in paper specification, and in its effects. American-specification 99s had all been re-tuned, with fuel-injection, to produce 110 bhp (compared with 118 bhp for the European-specification EMS), to meet the latest very tough exhaust emission laws, but the USA-specification turbocharged unit still produced 135 bhp (DIN) at 5000 rpm, and 160 lb ft torque at 3500 rpm, though the maximum boost was restricted to 0.5 bar (7 psi). For California only, the limits were even more strict, and Saab (like most other concerns) were forced to fit a catalytic converter in the exhaust system, under the floor. Saab engineers recently told me that a turbocharged engine makes it easier to meet exhaust emission limits at lower speeds, but that it was rather more difficult at the upper-end of the rev range. However, in the whole of the US cycle, they say, the turbocharger only actually begins to work on three occasions, while in the European cycle it

The fascia layout of the original 99 Turbo included a boost gauge mounted on its own separate pod on the crash roll, nearly in line with the driver's eyes. A padded steering wheel like this was normal to other 99s of the day

does not work at all!

No major changes were actually needed to the existing front-wheel-drive transmission to accommodate the extra Turbo torque, but to make the system even quieter than before the primary reduction drive was changed from a three-drop-gear arrangement (which had been used since the start of the project) to a Morse chain drive system. This was so arranged that there was a 0.9:1 ratio in the chain drive, so as the gearbox and final drives themselves were not changed, the overall gearing had been reduced by 10 per cent, to make the car even more lively than it might have been. The same basic change, incidentally, was made for all Saab transmissions to align them with the new, more refined, Turbo set-up.

At first, the 99 Turbo was only available with the three-door Combi-type body style, to which a variety of special cosmetic touches were applied. Those being passed by a 99 Turbo, or meeting one on the road, would be able to recognize it by the big air dam under the front bumper, by the spoiler at the base of the rear window, and by the new and very smart cast-alloy wheels, not forgetting the prominent 'Turbo' badges on the front wings, and on the front grille and rear tailgate. In any case this car was not likely to remain anonymous for long, as most of the cars seem to have been built in jet black (very sinister, and in the context of the 99 Turbo, very sexy as well) or, a special to Saab, bright red.

From the driving seat there was very little to tell a stranger that he was sitting behind a turbocharged engine. The fascia panel looked just like that of other 99s, except for the turbocharger boost gauge mounted in a pod on the crash roll, close to the windscreen pillar.

When I asked the engineers at Saab why they had chosen one particular position for the turbocharger itself (why was it to the right of the engine, and close to the radiator?) I was told that this was to cool the unit, and to aid the installation of full air conditioning under the bonnet—and did I know that every Turbo sold in North America had this feature?

Saab knew that their most difficult period would be at the beginning, when the press, and the first customers, came to terms with the behaviour of the engine. This was not an engine which felt like a sports-racing unit, for there was no obvious temperament, and no massive kick in the back when all the elements of turbocharging chimed in together at high revs. Instead, the Saab unit was smooth, civilized, and very progressive in its behaviour. Apart from the presence of the boost gauge in the driver's peripheral vision, and the fact that an experienced tester could pick up that exciting turbocharger whine as it wound up towards high operating speeds (Some customers were thrilled by the whine, but others irritated. Saab actually went to a great deal of trouble to minimize the whine, which they traced to out-of-balance forces in the rotor) the Turbo was a singularly civilized machine, with an exhaust note significantly quieter than the fuel-injection 99 EMS, and with all the comfortable trim, equipment, and safety features in place.

While it would not be true to suggest that it was the Saab Turbo which made turbocharging respectable in Europe (lead times are far too lengthy for the Saab to have any major effect on other turbocharged models produced in the next one or two years), it does seem to be true that the whole image of turbocharging began to improve thereafter. As Alan Allard has pointed out in his book on the technicalities of turbocharging: 'In 1977 there were only three turbocharged cars in production in the space of four years. By the end of 1980 this had increased to 18 models. . . .' For the new Saab Turbo was in very exalted, and exclusive company indeed.

The BMW 2002 Turbo had only lasted for one year, and after the Frankfurt Show of 1977 there were, quite literally, only four turbocharged cars on the market—the Saab being accompanied by the Porsche (930) Turbo, the Mercedes-Benz 300TD (which had a diesel engine) and the TVR Turbo (which was handbuilt, and really didn't count). As a series-production saloon, powered by petrol, and with civilized high performance, it was at that moment unique.

For the moment, however, there was only one

Side view of the 99 Turbo in 1978-model US-spec. form. There was barely an unfunctional line anywhere in this package, and the Americans just loved it. Come to think of it—they still do!

version of the Turbo on offer, though it would have been simple enough for the computerized assembly lines at Trollhättan to marry the Turbo engine/transmission pack to any of the body derivatives in the range. For the first year at least, each and every 99 Turbo would be built on the basis of the three-door Combi bodyshell (or Wagonback in the United States), almost to a standard specification.

Deliveries began almost at once; typical retail prices were $9998 in the USA, or £7850 (all taxes

*In North America, this is
how the press were told about
the new 99 Turbo model in
December 1977*

included) in Great Britain, and Saab's records show
that no fewer than 1066 Turbos were built before the
end of 1977, which confirmed that Saab were good
and ready to start selling the cars as soon as they
had launched the new model at Frankfurt. Saab,
who had built nearly 73,000 99s of all types in 1976,
but were only forecasting 60,000 in the current year,
collectively held their breath. Would the new car
not only boost the 99's performance, but also its
general sales appeal, and would it also improve
profitability, which had been sagging somewhat of
late?

They need not have worried. Almost everyone, it
seems, loved the new car. For the first time, here was
a Saab which need not be described as safe and well-
handling, but underpowered. For the first time, in
spite of what the company's publicists might
previously have said, here was a Saab which felt,
and performed, like a real performance car. In the
United States, where most of the early cars were
black, relieved only by touches of brightwork, the
Turbo took on the 'Darth Vader' image which had
sprung up so quickly following the release of the
film, *Star Wars*.

Saab's initial approach to marketing the car was
typified by the advertising set up in Great Britain at
the beginning of 1978. Headed 'Jet Black', a display
talked about 'The astonishing Saab Turbo.
Dramatically different in its all-black livery. And
packing an amazing turbocharged punch. . . . It's
like no other motor ever produced . . . the Saab
Turbo matches its power to a rugged practicality.
Its opulence to an unashamed economy. The
turbocharger only works when you want it to.
Cutting in with a monster surge of power for
overtaking or accelerating.'

The Turbo, incidentally, was not only the fastest
of the many different 99s, and the most expensive,
but it was also the best equipped of them all. It was

PRESS INFORMATION

SAAB-SCANIA OF AMERICA Inc. ● SAAB DRIVE ● ORANGE, CONNECTICUT 06477 ● 203 795-5671

FOR IMMEDIATE RELEASE   CONTACT: LEN LONNEGREN

SAAB TURBO SOON AVAILABLE THROUGH U.S. SAAB DEALERS
New Design for Performance and Economy has been widely tested

ORANGE, CONNECTICUT -- The new Saab Turbo, tested in over two million miles of driving under the most varying conditions, and already widely hailed by automotive experts the world over, will be available through the United States Saab dealers in early February.

A number of test prototypes of the revolutionary Saab Turbo have been on the road for over a year in Sweden, Germany, Switzerland and the United States, and have been driven at very high altitudes and at very high and very low temperatures. All tests have been designed to make sure that the Saab Turbo can function properly under these varying conditions.

Although turbo-charging has been used on motor vehicles for many years, for example on many high performance race cars, the Saab Turbo represents a new approach in this area.

The aim of the Saab Turbo project has been to obtain the best possible performance for everyday driving, while still retaining both good fuel economy and clean exhaust emissions. In effect, what the Saab Turbo designers have aimed for has been the performance of a considerably larger engine, without the larger powerplant's penalties in fuel economy. The turbo charger is there to provide extra power when needed during normal driving, such as when passing or when climbing long inclines.

something of a disappointment to the Saab
competitions department that the Turbo was not a
stripped-out, lightweight, road-burner—although
the car clearly had enormous potential in rallying,
as initially produced it would have to carry its own
weight and size handicap around for all to see.

It is interesting to recall just what sort of a price
premium was asked for Turbo performance, and I
intend to use early 1978 British prices for this
comparison. The down-market 99L two-door, with
the 100 bhp single-carburettor engine retailed for
£4150, whereas the three-door 118 bhp fuel injection
EMS cost £5985. The Turbo, on the other hand,
which included such features as a radio/cassette
unit, light alloy wheels, and £290-worth of sliding
sunroof as standard, cost £7850—31 per cent more
than the EMS.

The major breakthrough achieved by Saab was
that this was not a temperamental, inflexible,
racing-type turbocharged engine, but a massively
refined unit. As *Autocar* said in its first, frankly
eulogistic, road test of the car 'The Turbo is more
thrilling than even its advanced specification
suggests. It is not just its performance, but the way
the Turbo delivers it. Its acceleration pattern is
unique. Like a roller coaster running downhill, the
Saab just gets faster as the turbocharger boost
increases. It is an uncanny experience; the car's
acceleration starts quite modestly then builds up
dramatically as the boost increases. But the turbocharger is starting to operate from as low as 1500
rpm, so there is no sudden neck-snapping jerk
backward as it comes in, just a smooth, but very
impressive, build up of power.'

The magazine summarized the Turbo as 'One of
the most excitingly different cars on the market
today', which was exactly the effect which the
factory had always hoped to achieve. The next few
years were going to be very exciting for the Trolls.

Chapter 4
99s and 900s -
1977 onwards

No sooner had Saab astonished the world of motoring with their new turbocharged engine, than they did it all over again in 1978, this time with a new body style. Having up-rated their engines, and fleshed out a complete range of power units for the 1980s, they now produced the new shape of Saab which was to use them. The Saab 900 range, announced with such a flourish in May 1978, set the scene for the company's activities in the 1980s.

In the meantime, and before going on to describe the car which was so similar to the 99, but so different in many aspects, I ought to review what had been happening to Saab during the 1970s, and while the turbocharged engine was under development. Once the merger with Scania-Vabis had

900 Turbos for the British market in 1978/79, had the distinctive long-wheelbase/long-nose body shell, the massive bumpers, and the more delicate style of 'Turbo' badging on the front wings

matured (with Scania the major partner in terms of financial turnover), Saab-Scania AB found itself not only making Saab cars, and Scania trucks and buses, but building civil and military aircraft, distributing Audi, Porsche and VW products throughout Sweden, and beginning to get involved in more high-technology businesses including electronics, and the manufacture of steering systems for submarines. Saab-Scania also embraced distribution of Massey-Ferguson agricultural products, and—from 1976—there was a marketing agreement for Autobianchi cars which eventually developed into a design/development understanding with Lancia.

There was an awful lot going for Saab, and a great deal of hard thinking to be made about the company's future. Car assembly, which had been

Much detail thought went into every aspect of the 900 Turbo's styling and equipment. Those cast-alloy road wheels cannot have been cheap (those are Pirelli P6 tyres by the way), there was an entirely new dashboard, and the seats were furnished with extreme care. The interior of the 1979 3-door Turbos and EMS models were the same

almost entirely carried out at Trollhättan for the first 20 years, was now being carried out on three sites, for a new Finnish assembly plant on the shores of the Baltic was opened at Mystad in 1969, and in 1973 the first few cars were built in Belgium, at Mechelen, from kits supplied from Sweden. The Sonett sports coupés had been built at Arlov (one of the old railway company buildings) for some years, then 95 estate car assembly was moved there from Trollhättan in 1974, and eventually assembly of 99s was also started up in the same plant.

Even though sales had built up steadily throughout the 1970s (in 1974, when most motor manufacturers were suffering badly from the effects of the Suez war and the energy crisis, Saab-Scania's total sales increased from 5412 million Swedish Crowns to 6553 millions), the company thought it wise to talk seriously to Volvo when the Gothenburg car and truck manufacturing giant suggested a merger in 1977. In spite of the fact that it made little immediate 'dovetailing' sense (both concerns made large, versatile, and internationally-famous ranges of trucks and buses, and both made a wide range of medium-sized two-litre cars), all the options were considered before the idea was turned down.

There were short-lived fears that Saab might therefore be vulnerable, following the collapse of this proposed merger, but such critics cannot really have studied the company's accounts, which showed operating profits for 1976 of 336 million Swedish Crowns, in a year when 72,819 99s and 23,108 95s and 96s had been built. Saab might be smaller than Volvo, but it was no less confident, and no less secure.

When the three-door 99 Turbo, the original Turbo production car, was launched in the autumn of 1977, many of us suspected that other bodyshell derivatives would be made available with this engine, but I doubt if any journalist had an idea that Saab were also in the final stages of planning for a major re-style of their car—and one which would, in effect, produce a new model entirely. If they had followed the 'traditional' route of giving the new car

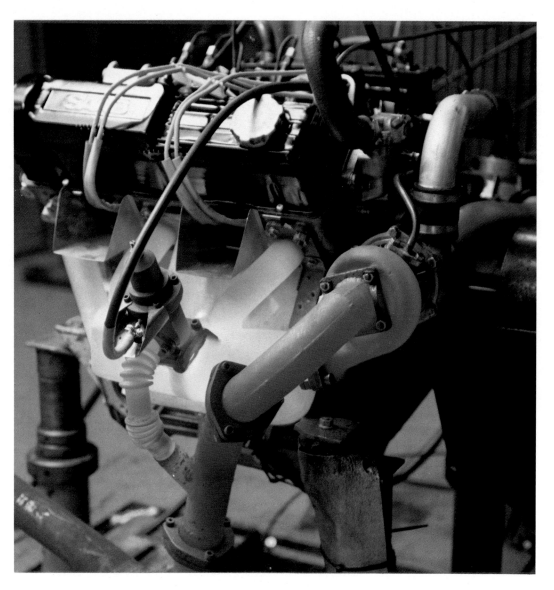

Saab have mastered the problem of excess heat generated by turbocharged engines. Here's what is possible on the test bench

Right *Most early 99 Turbos came to Britain in either Jet Black or in this subtle shade of 'poppy' red. Both choices suit the car's shape and successfully promote the right image*

Left *Road racing as opposed to rallying seems to have been most popular in North America for the Saab Turbo. Showroom Stock regulations make the Saab a front line contender. Successful Saab exponent Don Knowles in an early 99*

Left *A 1981 model 99 Turbo with add-on side stripe. The early 'rotor' style badge has already gone to be replaced with a more readable 'turbo'. These road wheels also symbolize the 'rotor'*

Right *1982 Saab 900 Turbo with three doors. Five speeds are also included. Note the revised wheels, Michelin TRX tyres and deep front air dam*

Far right *Only four doors, and automatic transmission. 1982 model to British specification*

Below *An American specification 3-door with the earlier 99 Turbo wheels (blackened) and a number of accessories such as a sun roof wind deflector and twin tail pipes*

Above *Italy is a curious
market for a Swedish product
but Saab 900 Turbos are
more common than one might
suppose. This is a Milan
registered 4-door. Note boot
spoiler and big-bore exhaust*

Right *On the road finds the
Turbo at its best. This is a 5-
door automatic. Dark colour,
very little bright work
contrast with Swedish
preference for permanent
running lights*

Left *The motor show at Birmingham in October 1982 gave the Finnish built 900 CD its first British airing. The description plaque calls it a 'director's car'*

Below *1983 model 5 door with APC and 5-speeds. America, of course, had APC as standard a little earlier. Magnificent*

the next project number in the sequence, the new car should have been the Saab 100, but this was not done. In a break with tradition, Saab chose to call their new model the 900, and that is how it met its public in 1978.

In preparation for the new car, there was a major reshuffle of facilities and assembly locations. The assembly facility in Belgium was closed down in 1978, and final assembly of all the surviving 99s was moved out of Trollhättan, to Arlov and to Mystad in Finland. To make room for *that* reshuffle, the last 95 estate cars and 96 V4 saloons were built at Arlov in 1978, while the last V4 saloons of all rolled off the Finnish factory production lines on 4 January 1980. The last of all was driven by Erik Carlsson straight to the company's museum at Trollhättan, while penultimate units went to concessionaires in Britain, Holland, Finland and West Germany.

The new 900, therefore, was to find its home at Trollhättan (though assembly from kits began in Finland almost at once), where the tooling facilities, particularly the highly automated ones concerning bodyshell assembly, were concentrated.

As a Saab publication about the 99s was headlined in 1975, their cars were 'Correctly conceived and properly built', which was a polite way of saying that Swedish thinking, and Swedish logic, had been brought to bear, whereas much of the excitement and emotion found in other makes had virtually been eliminated.

The 900 had evolved in much the same way. Saab had not only decided that they could not justify the time, effort, and expense of producing an entirely new bodyshell, but that they did not need one anyway. The 99, it was thought, had by no means outlived its appeal, so the 900 could be based on it— so closely, in fact, that the 99 could continue to be built with a fair proportion of common panelling being retained.

Identification parade? This was actually a 1979 model 3-door 900 Turbo, complete with Pirelli P6 tyres, and 145 bhp engine, registered for use in Sweden. Since there was really no easy way of 'picking' the rear of a 99 from a 900, the 900 Turbo had its model name mentioned on the hatchback itself

My good friend Michael Scarlett, *Autocar*'s technical editor, summarized the layout of the 900 perfectly, when he wrote this in the issue of 20 May 1978 'There is a strong family likeness [in the 900—AAGR] to the 99 Combi Coupe, which isn't so surprising since the centre and tail sections are basically the same. It is from forward of the A-post that things are obviously different from outside. Wheelbase lengthens by two inches, overall length goes up by 8.25 in. and there is a useful 4.7 in. more lengthwise space under the new low-line bonnet.'

The 900, in other words, was to be built as a three-door or a five-door car, using the same skins, centre and rear body work of the existing 99 Combis. This meant that the enormously useful tailgate feature was retained, and that for the five-door car there would still be those curious and small 'opera windows' in the quarters behind the rear passenger door. Under the car, there was redesigned rear suspension geometry, but because the car still had front wheel drive, it remained a 'dead' axle beam, with coil springs to provide suspension.

The radically new styling and engineering was at the front of the car, quite literally ahead of the 1.4 in. deeper windscreen. The new nose of the 900 was rendered more graceful because of the longer wheelbase—the wheels were further forward in relation to the screen and toeboard with no extra room for passengers—because of an even longer nose, and thanks to the rather more sweeping lines. The 900 was still recognizably a Saab, and still recognizably related to the 99, but it was somehow more sexy (if a car built by the logical-first Swedes can ever be that), and more up-market.

One reason for the extra length in the nose was to improve the overall 'balance' of the bodyshell (Combi versions of the 99 had always looked slightly 'stubby' ahead of the screen), but another was certainly to make the car more suitable to meet

*900 Turbos could be
persuaded to disappear very
rapidly indeed. By the time
the car reached the first
corner it would be exceeding
60 mph, and by the horizon ...*

Above *Right from the start 900 Turbos were available with a choice of bodies. This was the three-door, complete with a hatchback, while* Left *there was also the five-door, also with a hatchback, and complete with those unique rear quarter 'opera' windows, different wheels, and Michelin TRX tyres, all on the same floorpan and wheelbase*

Above *Arguably the best tyres in the world, Michelin TRX, on the 1979 5-door 900 Turbo*

Below *The engine room of the 1979 900 Turbo, shot from above the windscreen*

barrier crash and other safety regulations, particularly in North America. When the author saw how much more space there was in the engine bay he instantly assumed that a longer, or alternative engine, was also on the way, but such a development has not yet appeared, and will probably not do so.

In fact the front suspension was much like that of the 99, though the rack and pinion steering had been relocated, and power assistance was to be standard on GLE and turbocharged models. The engines to be offered in the 900s were all, naturally, of the usual 1985 cc size, with ratings of 100 bhp (single carburettor) 108 bhp (twin Zenith-Stromberg carburettors), 118 bhp (Bosch fuel injection) and 145 bhp (with turbocharging), and were the same as those used in 99s in almost every respect.

The transmission under the engines was much as before, though as far as the Turbos were concerned the choice of tyres was complicated—three-door cars were to be equipped with 195/60HR-15 in. low-profile Pirelli P6 rubber, while the five-door versions were treated to the new and very advanced 180/65HR-390 mm Michelin TRX tyres, which required their own special metric-diameter light alloy wheels.

The major advances in the 900, compared with the 99, were in its fittings and equipment. The feature which made all the headlines was the ducting of all air for the passenger compartment through a replaceable cartridge filter, claimed to trap particles larger than two microns (about 8/100,000th in.), which meant that dust, pollen and about 50 per cent of airborne bacteria could be excluded. The 900, in fact, was the world's first 'hay-fever special', and this feature was reputedly inspired by the fact that one of the senior development chiefs suffered severely from that affliction.

There was a striking, and ergonomically very efficient, new fascia design and instrument display, in which the installation of full air conditioning (so very important to the prospects of any new car in North America) was very neatly incorporated. No 900 driver, surely, could complain that he was lacking information now!

By this time, therefore, the line-up of 99s and 900s was looking distinctly complicated—and this was only at the start of the 900's life. When the 900 was 'leaked' some months before sales and series production were due to begin, there were twelve 99s, and six new 900s. However, help for bewildered Saab dealers was at hand, for once the 900s went on sale, many of the existing 99s were dropped. Basically, and apart from old stock being cleared through the showrooms, by 1979 only two-door and four-door 99s were being built, these effectively being bottom-of-the-range cars, with the most costly and better-equipped 900s taking over as three-door and five-door models.

It is time, therefore, to work out and show just what happened to the turbocharged cars in 1978 and 1979—not by any means an easy task.

The original 99 Turbo of October 1977 was a three-door Combi, and this was joined by a closely related five-door version during 1978. Neither of these derivatives was built for very long (even in the UK, where there was considerable 'pipeline' effect delaying deliveries from Sweden, the last were imported at the beginning of 1979, only nine months after the original launch) even though they were price-listed for many months after that.

In the meantime, not only to keep the factory competitions department happy, but to provide a somewhat cheaper version of the turbocharged Saab than the plushy 900-based machines, a two-door saloon 99 Turbo was launched at the beginning of 1979, and marketed until 1981. Mechanically, of course, this car was identical with the other 99 Turbos, but it had the rather less bulky (and,

For 1980 the 900 Turbo was treated to a five-speed gearbox, which made it even more versatile than before. For the USA, as before, it still had 135 bhp

therefore, less heavy) saloon body style without a hatchback.

The 900 Turbos went on sale in the autumn of 1978, along with all the other derivatives of that new body style, so by the autumn of 1979 the line up of 145 bhp Turbos (135 bhp for USA customers, of course) was:

99 2-door saloon, weight approx. 2490 lb, length 14 ft 6 in.

900 3-door Combi coupé, weight approx. 2650 lb, length 15 ft 6.5 in.

900 5-door Combi coupé, weight approx. 2650 lb, length 15 ft 6.5 in.

The 99 2-door did not have power-assisted steering whereas the 900s did, along with other extra items of equipment. Here in the UK, therefore, this helps to explain the prices which obtained at the time of the launch of the 2-door 99 Turbo, which were:

99 2-door	£7750
900 3-door	£9910
900 5-door	£10,310

--and it is worth pointing out that the original 99 3-

Below left Saab's 99 and 900 range is unique, with the ignition key/starter switch on the tunnel behind the gear-lever. When operating, the transmission/gear-lever lock is almost unbreakable.

Below 1980 model 900 Turbos had a revised interior and different seat styles

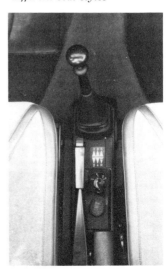

door Turbo had cost £7850 when launched in the UK in the spring of 1978.

In the next few years, development work on the turbocharged engine and transmission was concentrated on the 900 Turbo, while the surviving two-door 99 Turbo merely picked up these changes as they came along; at all times Saab had to remember that their biggest single market was the United States, and that the competition they faced in that continent was always intense.

As far as the USA was concerned, it was always necessary to remember that customers treated the 900 Turbo as a 'clean' and safe high-performance saloon, and that even though there was a nation-wide speed limit of 55 mph in force (widely ignored, but equally as widely enforced by the highway patrol), the Turbo had to have really outstanding acceleration. It was for this reason, therefore, that Saab offset the loss in peak power and torque imposed by exhaust emission controls, by making the USA-market Turbos slightly lower geared. This was done, not by altering the final drive ratio (which would have been expensive), but by changing the primary chain transfer ratio instead; this was easily done by altering the number of teeth on one of the triple-chain drive sprockets.

For the record, the final drive and step down ratios were as follows in 1979:
European: Final drive 3.89:1 (35/9 teeth); Chain ratio 0.839:1, overall ratio 3.264:1
USA: Final drive 3.89:1 (35/9 teeth); Chain ratio 0.9:1, overall ratio 3.501:1

The first, and very important, change to the specification of the 900 Turbo came along for 1980, when a five-speed gearbox was made available, but not standardized for all markets. Small changes were needed to the under-engine casing to persuade the five-speed cluster into place, but the general layout of the transmission layout was not com-

The plushy four-door 900 Turbo of 1980 had yet another variation on the theme which Saab had started with the 99 in 1969. I should make it clear that the 900's four-door tail was entirely different from that of the 99's four-door tail. Nose, floorpan, screen and all four doors were the same as that of the five-door version. Borg-Warner automatic transmission became optional for 1981

In 1981 this was the Turbo engine in 'H' form, one recognition point being the distributor on the end of the camshaft cover

pletely redesigned—in other words the drive was still taken from the front of the engine, there was a transfer to the gearbox by triple row chain, the box was under and ahead of the centre line of the engine, and the final drive itself was under the engine itself. The three rows of Renold's chain, incidentally, are to the same age-old pitch which the British concern have used for so long, but are slightly staggered relative to each other so as to cut the noise problem even further, and the transmission has its own separate supply of lubricant, and does not share it with the hard-working engine.

Technically-minded readers will know, I am sure, that there are 'easy' and 'not-so-easy' ways of developing a five-speed gearbox, if the basic layout of an existing four-speed box is to be retained. The 'easy' way is to tack an overdrive fifth gear on to the existing cluster—the 'not-so-easy' way is to rework the transmission from end to end. Need I say, therefore, that Saab, as professionals and meticulous engineers, did the job properly?

Saab wanted to achieve two things—one was to

In 1981 Saab 900 Turbo interiors looked like this (the four-door body style is featured), and the fascia panel was as comprehensive as would have been expected from Saab. Unlike the 99 the turbo boost gauge is neatly incorporated

raise the overall gearing (to give more restful high-speed cruising and better potential operating economy), and the other was to provide more idealized gearing to make the most of the Saab's performance. With a five-speed gearbox, this was achieved by specifying an even higher primary chain transfer ratio, by retaining an otherwise 'direct' top (i.e. fifth gear) ratio, and dropping the bottom gear ratio to compensate for this. All the intermediate ratios were re-jigged to suit.

It sounds more complex than it was, but this was the overall effect on gearing:
Gear ratios, four-speed: 3.693, 2.194, 1.472, 1.000, reverse 4.002. Final drive 3.89:1. Chain 0.839:1.
Gear ratios, five-speed: 4.25, 2.562, 1.72, 1.236, 1.00, reverse 4.675. Final drive 3.89:1. Chain 0.781:1.

The overall gears apparent to a driver were:
Four-speed: 12.05, 7.12, 4.80, 3.264, reverse 13.06:1

In 1981, the 900 Turbo four-door announced its departure with a rubberized spoiler on the boot lid (this had not featured on the car revealed a little earlier), and the badging indicated that a five-speed gearbox was also standard

Five-speed: 12.91, 7.78, 5.23, 3.75, 3.038, reverse
14.20:1

For 1980, therefore, a Saab Turbo enthusiast had
many alternatives to consider before he placed his
order. He could have 2-door 99, 3-door 900 or 5-door
900 models, four- or five-speed manual gearboxes in
some countries, and the teasing choice of P6 tyres
(3-door) or TRX tyres (5-door), coupled with the
chance to specify full air-conditioning into the
bargain.

But Saab had by no means exhausted the
possibilities for change with the new 900s. Not only
were they planning to introduce (or re-introduce, if
the truth was told) yet another body derivative, but
they also had yet another transmission variant in
mind, and a considerably modified engine too! As far
as the 900 Turbos were concerned, all these changes
were introduced together in the autumn of 1980, for
the start-up of the 1981 model-year.

*The 1981 version of the Saab
900's nose, including
headlamp wipe/wash, air
ducts to the front brakes, and
Michelin TRX tyres on all
models*

In the search for greater efficiency and reduced weight, Saab's now-famous 2.0-litre slant-four engine was thoroughly re-designed, and became known as the 'H' type unit. The distributor was repositioned on the die-cast valve gear cover (and driven off the camshaft), while the oil pump was integrated into the front timing cover, the fuel pump by a cam from the camshaft and the water pump by the alternator drive belt. Not only could the layout of the cylinder block be simplified, but it could be made stiffer and lighter—the net result being that 11.5 kg/25.4 lb weight was saved, and the unit became between two and three per cent more efficient.

At the same time, on the turbocharged engines, a new type of integrated wastegate controlled by intake manifold pressure, was introduced to replace the original exhaust-pressure poppet-valve variety. There were no changes to peak power and torque ratings as a result of these improvements.

The new gearbox option was that of the fully-

By 1982 the three-door 900 Turbo looked more chunky even than before, and sales seemed to be going up with every year which passed

automatic three-speed Borg-Warner gearbox, which had always been available on non-turbocharged 900s ever since they were announced in 1978. Because the Saab had front-wheel-drive, the conventional type of Borg-Warner installation could not be used. However, the British-based company had already performed similar space utilization miracles for Citroën (with the DS) and BL (with the 1800s and 2200s), so the problem had not been new to them. It meant, however, that the usual torque converter was at the front of the engine where the manual clutch would normally be, and that the complex three-speed gearing had to be under the engine where Saab's normal manual gearbox was located. To match the transmission, and its inherent slight power losses, yet another primary chain transfer ratio was chosen—this time, 0.968, which resulted in an overall top gear ratio of 3.764:1.

The body derivative was actually unveiled at the Geneva Motor Show of March 1980, and was a conventional four-door saloon, though its use was confined to turbocharged cars for the first few months. However, the 900 four-door Sedan, as Saab called it, was not merely the front of the 900 with the old centre and tail sections of the old 99 four-door saloon. Instead, the new car was identical with other 900s as far back as the B/C pillar behind the front doors. The rear doors resembled also those of the five-door cars, but it was an altogether more graceful tail section which incorporated a curving rear window, and the tail lamps looked similar to those fitted to 900 hatchbacks. A measure of the difference was that the boot floor was nearly three inches longer in this car than it had been in the four-door 99, and there was now space for the spare wheel to be safely stowed flat underneath.

There were, however, several other changes and improvements for 1981, of which the most techni-

Saab 900 production at Trollhättan. Some days one in every three 900s assembled has the turbocharged engine

A variation on a familiar layout—this is a British-market 900 Turbo five-door, with sun-roof open, and with automatic transmission

cally significant was that first and reverse gears were lowered on four- and five-speed transmissions, to give an even quicker step-off from rest, and better steep hill-climbing capabilities. In addition there were new front seat mountings, extra space in the rear seat, new smaller steering wheels with four spokes, and on turbocharged cars an increase in fuel tank capacity from 55 to 63 litres (12.1 to 13.9 Imp. gallons). Finally, the tyre specification of all 900 Turbos—three-, four- *and* five-door—was standardized; henceforth, all of them would have 180/65HR390 Michelin TRX rubber on the special metric diameter rims.

A small change also introduced at this time was that a smaller turbocharger was standardized, with

different characteristics. Once again, there were no changes in advertized ratings, but it was done to reduce turbo 'lag' even further, and hence to make the engine even more responsive than before to abrupt throttle opening from low engine speeds.

The line-up of body styles was now complete (and the two-door 99 Turbo, let's not forget, was dropped at the end of the 1980 model year), but there were still more improvements to come for 1982. Yet again Saab had been juggling their transmission ratios; having lowered first and reverse gears for 1981, they now modified the driveline again by raising the final drive for 1982, and juggling the primary chain ratios to suit. For 1982, therefore, these became

Gear ratios, four-speed: 3.882, 2.194, 1.472, 1.000, reverse 4.271. Final drive 3.667:1. Chain 0.9:1.

Gear ratios, five-speed: 4.533, 2.562, 1.719, 1.236, 1.000, reverse 4.987. Final drive 3.667:1. Chain 0.839:1.

At the same time, the Turbos were equipped with centralized door and boot lid locking as standard.

As far as the 'first generation' Saab Turbos is concerned, the development story is now complete, though the prospect for the new 'second generation' cars, now equipped with APC (Automatic Performance Control) is even more enthralling. I describe this breakthrough in engine management techniques in a later chapter.

Clearly, the Saab Turbo concept had succeeded to an even greater degree than the company had hoped, for sales increased every year from 1977 to 1982. In the 1982 model year, almost 20,000 Turbos of all types were built—which meant that well over 400 such cars were leaving Trollhättan in an average week. The Turbo was a splendid car, of course, but part of this popularity was certainly due to the reputation it was given by the technical press. In the first few years, they gave the cars unanimous praise.

Chapter 5
Turbo tests – what the critics think

It was one of those introductions which company PR men dream about. There wasn't a country, or a magazine, which didn't enthuse about the 99 Turbo—and there was really so much favourable comment that Saab needed to do very little advertising of their own. The message, though, was of a new 'Superswede', which tied in well with what some testers said of the car, and with the image of Bjorn Borg, who was then at the height of his powers.

Almost without exception, testers seemed to take the 99's familiar virtues as read, and concentrated on the new turbocharged engine and the performance. After all, they already knew about the massively strong body, the stability of the front-

The last of the 99 Turbos was the two-door model, distinctly and definitely down-market from the 900s. It was also somewhat lighter, which made it ideal for use by the factory competitions department

Above *The rear quarter view of the two-door 99 Turbo shows that its presswork was the same as earlier 99s, but entirely different from that given to the four-door 900. Even the Swedes let style get in the way of practicality at times*

Right *A well-used pre-H-Series turbo installation in the less spacious 99 engine bay*

wheel-drive handling, and the safety-conscious equipment and specifications.

Autocar's comments, already mentioned, were mirrored fairly accurately by other magazines. *Road & Track* of North America headlined their test: 'Honing an exceptional car to an even finer edge', and went on to say that: 'When we road tested the Saab Turbo we said that it is so much fun to drive that the price is irrelevant. . . .' But the price *was* relevant, for in North America it stood at $9998 for the three-door in mid-1978, and that was an extremely attractive proposition.

John Bolster of *Autosport*, who likes to be nice about a car if he possibly can, succinctly headed his analysis 'Car of the Future'. His text described the car as exciting, and he was at pains to say that 'High cornering power is a feature and, like all Saabs, the behaviour of wet roads is outstanding.' He was very charitable indeed about the steering, but did not think it over-heavy; almost all testers on the other hand, thought the manual steering too

Some testers were not very complimentary about the instrument layout of the first 99 Turbos, particularly the rather 'afterthought' mounting of the turbo boost gauge

heavy, a criticism speedily dealt with, for power-assisted steering was to be a standard feature on the larger, and later, 900 Turbo.

There were, as expected, eulogies about the sheer urge available, but Bolster's most significant remarks were in the summary 'It is difficult to put into words the charm and fascination of this remarkable car. As a combination of performance, refinement, and fuel economy, it stands alone, and the integrity of its engineering and the quality of its finish are second to none. If you were to conclude from the above that this is just about the best motor car which is at present being made, anywhere, you wouldn't be far wrong.'

Heady stuff, and one would be tempted to dismiss it as hyperbole if only other people hadn't said much the same thing in different ways. Even Clive Richardson, writing in *Motor Sport*, a British

Motoring is international in the 1980s. This three-door five-speed Turbo, built in Sweden, is on test in Italy, and is carrying Turin number plates. Saab, don't forget, are getting together with Lancia on new-model design in the mid-1980s!

magazine which can be as sour as a jilted prune if it takes a dislike to anything, called the car 'Quite an Experience'. Richardson, reminding his readers of the 'almost unprecedented eulogistic descriptions in some of the weekly journals earlier in the year', pointed out that the first car presented to him for test was not good, but that the second machine, on which he was now commenting, was much better. He told everyone that the Turbo could feel slow, and disappointing if trundled around, but 'Floor the throttle and the chameleon quality takes over in the most astonishing fashion. As the boost builds up, accompanied by a shrill whistle that is not normal on a Saab Turbo, in my experience—AAGR], the car rapidly gains momentum with a smoothness and quietness that can be totally deceptive . . . what is so staggering is the manner in which the speed rises incessantly, in top gear in particular, like the

Left *A bonnetful of engineering for testers to enthuse over (this being a 1982 900 Turbo, complete with TRX tyres and H-type engine), and* above *the small but neat rev-counter showing a warning sector beginning at 5500 rpm, and a 'danger' sector in red at 6000 rpm*

brightening of theatre lights by a rheostat.' He thought it was '. . . a modern day wonder for mass production motor cars.'

Even so, *Motor Sport* soon picked up the problem of so much available torque on a front-wheel-drive car on slippery roads: 'It is all too easy to provoke wheelspin through all three lower gears if conditions are slippery and this can be accompanied by very twitchy torque reaction and side to side snatching which needs a firm hand on the wheel to control. The throttle needs treating with respect in the wet or on the loose, therefore, especially when coming out of slippery, tight, corners: if the turbocharger happens to come in at the wrong moment with lock applied the torque reaction makes it difficult to unwind the lock. The result at best can be a snaky recovery or at worst terminal understeer.'

In general, long-term owners never got bored with their cars, for the charms of such performance never wear off. *Road & Track* kept a three-door 99 Turbo as a staff car for 24,000 miles, and at the end of this they said that 'nothing about it is ordinary', and

that it was 'The most entertaining long-term car we've tested.'

But were we (and I say 'we', because I was one of those who loved the Saab Turbo after my first drive in one) all *too* enthusiastic about the car? Perhaps I should let the final word on the original 99 Turbo go to Mel Nichols of *Car*, the British monthly which continues to infuriate the motor industry by its unorthodox views on the world of motor cars. Nichols headed his review 'Part time tiger—or little lamb lost?', and among his words were 'Inevitably it falls to CAR to penetrate the aura of ecstacy that has surrounded this motoring enigma, this vehicle that is as two-faced as Janus . . . it has shaken the dust off this far-from-conservative company's image. . . .

'Even if Saab made not a reindeer's antler from the Turbo it would still go down in the company's books as the master-stroke of the 1970s. . . .

'The Turbo is a fast—very fast—car by any standards. . . . The horses come pouring in to deliver acceleration in a swift, smooth and steady surge . . .

'. . . overtaking requires engine-transmission

In the author's view, the side aspect of the five-door 900 is too fussy, with all those windows, bulges, and air extractors. Would it look better without those silly little 'opera' windows, perhaps? Testers' views were varied

A British 900 Turbo on test in 1982—the Oxfordshire registration tells us that it is an importer's demonstration car

management. Without it, you can find yourself on the wrong side of the road—waiting.'

During that long-weekend in a three-door 900 Turbo which Saab (GB) kindly lent me during 1982, I was constantly reminded of those words from Mel Nichols. It was one of those summer weekends when I needed to make several fast journeys, and some leisurely ones. There was a sun-roof, the weather was warm, and it was so very easy not to be completely alert.

It was true—the Turbo *is* a part-time tiger. Trundling around in towns in a long line of traffic can convince the driver that the turbocharger is not fitted, or not working, because below about 2000 rpm (still more than 30 mph in fifth gear) there is no boost at all. At those speeds, and in those con-

In styling terms, perhaps the most integrated of all the 900 Turbos—this four-door model is a 1982 example

ditions, the 900 Turbo felt like an overweight, and underpowered, family car.

But not for long. Slip past the derestriction sign, change down at least two gears, and . . . the tiger slips its leash. The needle on the boost gauge whips round, the nose twitches upwards, and the car simply leaps off towards the horizon. Even more so in the 900 Turbo, which has five gears, than in the 99 Turbo, it is quite possible to arrive at corners, or traffic hazards, going 20 or 30 mph too fast; it's on occasions like that when the power-assisted four-disc brake installation system was appreciated.

Perhaps John Bolster was going over the top when he suggested that the 99 Turbo might just be the best motor car being made in 1978, and in later years he was certainly wrong, as the Saab turbocharged concept was copied by others—but the later development of the theme, the 900 Turbo, was still a car which reaped a lot of praise. *Autocar*'s test of the five-door model was headlined: 'A distinct refinement' and the point was made that the Turbo's engine behaved just like that of a highly-tuned unit, normally aspirated, but that there was none of the temperament: 'There is the same lack of go at the bottom end, the same joyous eruption into full life further on—but with the very important difference from the driveability viewpoint that the turbo engine is perfectly smooth below the lively region, with not the slightest hint of the sports engine's coughing and spluttering.'

In April 1979, *Road & Track* were quite outspoken. They merely called the 900 Turbo the: 'Blending the best of the 99 into an exceptional new car'. The fact that their test car had power steering, automatically heated driver's seat, and a typically efficient Scandinavian-style heater for a test carried out during a snowy spell, all helped. But prices were leaping in the United States, as well as in Britain and the rest of Western Europe. *R & T*'s five-door, which achieved 114 mph even in de-toxed form, retailed at $11,968. For 1980 that price had leapt by a further $1000.

Road & Track summarized the whole appeal of a Saab to the Americans in a sign-off paragraph to a test published in 1980, which encapsulates the appeal of the car to so many enthusiasts. 'Saab's approach to automobiles is markedly different: from the exterior styling to the interior appointments, there's no mistaking it for any other car. And while perhaps that has been detrimental to sales success among the general population and those seeking the comfort of anonymity, it has endeared the Swedish carmaker to its fiercely loyal *aficionados*. For them, and us, the Saab Turbo means comfort, sure handling, and driving excitement.'

Chapter 6
APC and beyond - science and the Black Art

Getting extra power from a turbocharged engine is one thing, but making it manageable power is another. To produce the sheer untamed urge is relatively easy, but getting rid of turbo 'lag', taming the combustion characteristics, and making the car refined and easy to drive is something else. From the very beginning, Saab realized that there was potential locked inside their own engine which could not be used.

The engineers I consulted say that the original 145 bhp/174 lb ft settings were a compromize, one leaving adequate reserves of strength in the transmission, giving sparkling performance with an acceptable lag, and sufficient margin over the 'knocking', or pre-ignition, tendency which is present in all high-performance engines. But it was all very frustrating—they were sure that they could improve the installation still further, given time.

The main opportunity seemed to be to improve engine control by some form of knock detection, so that the engine could operate at its maximum efficiency at all times. That way, it was thought, acceleration, driveability and fuel economy could all be optimized.

Conventional thinking said that knock had to be controlled by some form of retarded ignition, but Saab decided to tackle the job by controlling the turbocharger boost through a variable wastegate setting. When knock was about to set in, they

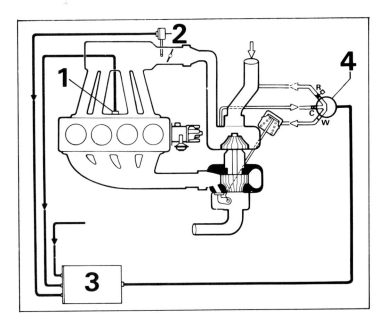

Non-technical readers should skip this page, for the drawing (top) and the dismantled components (below) explain the layout and function of the APC control, now standard on all 900 Turbos. Basically, it is sophisticated engine control to eliminate 'knocking', and make the engine compatible with all grades of petrol. 1) Is the knock detector on the block, 2) the inlet manifold pressure transducer, 3) the control unit stripped in the lower picture, and 4) the solenoid valve modulating the turbocharger wastegate control

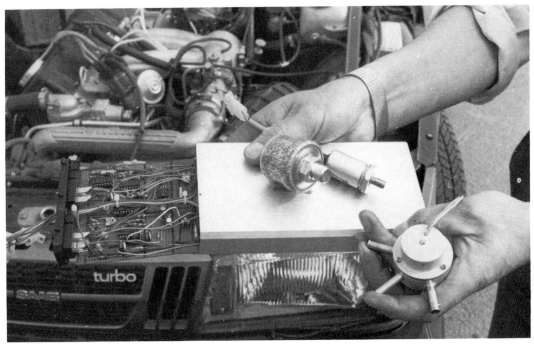

Above *The 1983-model turbocharged unit, complete with APC control*

Below *By 1983 the engine bay was full of engine, componentry and control gear, to which the APC control was an added factor*

wanted to turn down the boost (in domestic terms, that was like turning down the heat under a pan of milk just as soon as it shows a tendency to boil over)—and they wanted this to be a continuous monitoring of the engine's performance. The secret of success, they reasoned, was to use electronic controls, and a system which would 'cycle' (or repeat its function) very quickly indeed.

Work began in 1979, and progress was astonishingly quick by motor industry standards. Success came so fast that Saab were able to patent their findings worldwide, in the spring of 1980; it was such that Per Gillbrand could read a learned paper to the Society of Automotive Engineers in Detroit in June 1980. Broad-scale testing of 60 test cars began in North America and various European territories at about the same time, and by May 1981 the system was not only proven, but finalized. The first production cars thus equipped were supplied to North America in May 1982, and all Turbos were uprated to the new 'second generation' type of engine for the 1983 model year.

Saab's new system was known as APC, or Automatic Performance Control, and consisted of four principal elements. To the basic turbocharged engine as we know it was added a knock detector measuring vibration in the engine (this was positioned on the engine block on the inlet manifold side near the cylinder head face), a pressure sensor in the inlet tract to measure the pressure in the inlet manifold on the way to the engine, and a solenoid valve controlling the limits of that induction charge pressure by operating on the turbocharger's wastegate. These elements were monitored, and the whole system controlled by solid-state electronics.

In modern technological terms, the rest is easy. If the Saab Turbo engine tends to knock, or detonate, the sensor tells the electronic box of tricks, which is also monitoring the pressure of the fuel/air mixture

in the inlet passage; thus warned, it instantly commands the solenoid valve to lift the wastegate valve, which reduces the pressure, and therefore eliminates the knock. Simple? Simple to say, indeed, and relatively simple to understand when looking at an engine, but not at all easy to put into practice. When I merely point out that the APC installation can make adjustments up to 12 times *a second*, the sophistication of the components (and their light inertia) becomes clear.

It was the sort of breakthrough which other car makers had been looking for all over the world. Saab were soon being approached, not only to sell their expertise, but to supply complete engines for other manufacturers to use. It was with some pride that Saab received an approach from one very famous manufacturer, with a world-wide reputation for the excellence of their own engine design, but for the moment they are keeping the development to themselves.

For 1983, therefore, all Turbos not only get APC,

The 1982 US-market 900 Turbo not only had APC engine control—the much-vaunted 'second generation' turbocharged engine—but new-style wheels, and the turbo boost gauge reminded the driver of the APC control by this discreet mark on the dial

but they get a camshaft profile now common with all other 900s. On the USA-market cars it has been possible to raise the unblown compression to 8.5:1, and get boost pressure up from the previous setting of 0.5 Bar to 0.65 Bar. Even the Californian-spec cars are now exactly the same as those for all other North American states.

But APC was not the only change, or addition, made to the range of Turbo cars for 1983. Publicity *coups* like the use of a 900 Turbo as the new James Bond car in *Licence Renewed*, written by John Gardner, did the car no harm at all, and the news that the 200,000th 900 model had been built in June 1982 merely proved that many of the world's motorists liked the type of car which a modest little concern in Sweden was prepared to sell them.

The most interesting development, however, had already been previewed in September 1981, when the Finnish Saab associate company were entrusted with the job of building specially lengthened versions of the four-door 900 Turbo, to be called 900 CD models, for export market. These had been for home consumption only, at first, but were offered on other markets before the end of 1982.

A Saab 900 CD looks almost the same as the normal four-door saloon—until, that is, one realizes that the wheelbase is somewhat longer, and that all the increase has been arranged to give larger front and rear doors, and a lot more rear seat room. The wheelbase and leg-room improvement, in fact, was 20 cm/7.9 in., which meant that the car's overall length went up by the same amount, and that there was a weight penalty of about 30 kg/66 lb.

Because the 900 CD was a somewhat specialized type of car, it had Borg-Warner automatic transmission as standard, special extra reading lamps in the back seat, foot cushions, and provision for a radio/telephone console to be added. In addition, the 900 CD received other development touches

Above *This, no doubt, is the most exclusive 900 Turbo of all, the long-wheelbase 900 CD, built for Saab by the Finnish associate company, and now on sale outside Scandinavia*

Below *Much of the increased interior space in the long-wheelbase 900 CD was in the rear seat compartment*

shared with the other Turbos for 1983, which included the use of central locking for all models, bronze-tinted window glass, a new centre console, different types of upholstery, and (very significant, this) the use of asbestos-free disc brake pads on all Saabs which not only increased the potential life of the pads, and improved braking performance in ice and snow but eliminated the medically chilling prospect of asbestos dust being generated around the car.

At the Geneva Motor Show of March 1983, however, Saab astonished the world of motoring by unveiling their third generation of turbocharged engines—this time a more powerful 16-valve twin-cam unit with great potential for the future. As I have already pointed out, it would be difficult to enlarge the H-Type engine by more than about 200 cc, but Saab were convinced that they needed more power and torque in the 1980s. The only way to achieve this without increasing boost pressure was to make the engine breathe more efficiently.

The new unit, still only in prototype form, and

In 1983, the 900 Turbo three-door had sleek new wheels, and could be supplied in this Special Equipment guise. Under the skin, of course, APC control was standard

due to be subjected to broad-based testing in 50 cars over at least 1.8 million miles in 1983 and 1984, featured a 16 valve cylinder head (four valves per cylinder—two inlet and two exhaust), and twin overhead camshafts. The new head looked similar to, but was quite different from, that used in normally-aspirated rally 99s in the late 1970s. Not only were the camshafts driven by chain, as for all 'normal' Turbos, but the inverted bucket-type tappets featured hydraulic valve lifters, which added to the overall refinement of the unit.

The 16-valve unit was claimed not only to be more powerful, but more economical than the conventional engine. Saab pointed out that if they added an intercooler to the specification of the engine, up to 180 bhp (and a transient 200 bhp for 'snap' overtaking) was available. However, the first stage featured no inter-cooler, and an easily-attained 160 bhp at 5500 rpm, with peak torque of 177 lb ft at 3000 rpm; this compares with 145 bhp at 5000 rpm, and 171 lb ft torque at 3000 rpm with the conventional 8-valve engine.

The interior of the 1983 Special Equipment model— here seen as the three-door— had leather seating

The compression ratio (nominal, that is) had been raised to 8.5:1, an indication of the improved anti-knock capabilities of the pent-roof combustion chamber layout, and the latest type of Bosch LH electronic fuel injection was specified. One benefit of these changes, which not only gave more power, but more efficient combustion, was that the fuel consumption of the unit was actually lowered—Saab claimed a 10 per cent power uprating *and* a 10 per cent reduction in fuel consumption.

Even though they were still effectively a 'one-product' (or, at least, a 'one-engine' business), and not at all represented at the economy-car end of the price scale anywhere in the world, Saab's sales were standing up remarkably well. In 1981, for example, Saab held 13.8 per cent of the Swedish market, while in North America their sales were surging ahead at a time when domestic manufacturers were struggling even to stay in business. It was an achievement set up by the maturing of a solid reputation, and the joyful use of competitions to further their image. In the last 20 years or so, there had been many wins.

Even as the first edition of this book went to press, Saab surprised the world with their 'third generation' Turbo engine—this time with a twin-camshaft *16-valve cylinder head, incorporating hydraulic tappets. Peak power is up from 145 bhp (8-valve version) to 160 bhp (16-valve twin-cam version). Production was expected in 1984, after broad-scale testing of 60 development cars*

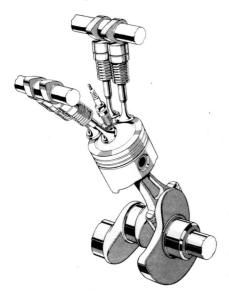

Chapter 7
Racing and rallying the Turbo

The Turbo came on the scene at exactly the right time for the Saab factory competitions department. Not only were they looking for more power—and more manageable power, at that—for their 99s, but they were also faced with the imminent loss of their existing high-performance options. The timing was akin to that demonstrated in all the class Western movies—that when all seems lost, the cavalry comes galloping over the hill to save the day. The arrival of the Turbo was just as timely as that.

'Works' Saabs had been winning international rallies since the mid-1950s, and had become world-famous along with the rise to fame of that giant of a man, Erik Carlsson. Two-stroke 93s and 96s had given way to the re-engined Saab V4s in 1967, but by the early 1970s these gallant cars were being outgunned by more specialized machines from Ford, Lancia, Alpine-Renault and Porsche.

The 99, although first produced in 1968, and investigated by the competitions department in 1970 and 1971, was not officially used in an event until 1974. By 1975 a team car was ready for use with a twin-Weber conversion of its standard single-cam 2.0-litre engine. It was quite clear that it was not going to be an outright winner, particularly because the 99 was such a bulky machine. So for 1976 Saab announced a very special engine kit, which comprised a twin-overhead-camshaft cylinder head with four valves per cylinder.

This was done in the happy days when the rules of homologation allowed makers to offer 'alternative cylinder heads', of which only 100 examples had to be built if the cars were running in Appendix J Group 2. Saab, at least, were more honest than some of their rivals, for they actually built 100 kits, and offered them for sale at a very high price, though when I was at Trollhättan in 1982 I was told that stocks of this kit were *still* in existence at the factory!

No sooner had Saab produced this kit, and started to win events with it, than the rules were changed. At the end of 1977, the concession of alternative heads was to be withdrawn, which meant that makers of true Supercars like Ford (with their RS1800) and Fiat (with their 131 Abarth) would have an even greater advantage than before.

This was a bitter blow for Saab, whose 220 bhp 99 EMS models, though heavy, and with an extremely peaky torque delivery, had proved to be competitive. Stig Blomqvist had won the Boucles de Spa on the 16-valve unit's very first outing in February 1976, but probably an even better achievement was for him to take second place in the 1976 Lombard-RAC Rally, just 4 m 37 sec behind Roger Clark's flying Ford Escort RS. In 1977 there was good and bad news, for the 16-valve EMSs won the Finnish Arctic and the Swedish, but failed in the 1000 Lakes and the Lombard-RAC.

No matter. Team manager Bo Hellberg had, at least, had sufficient warning of the banning of the 16-valve engine for 1978, and as he was privy to the secrets of the design and development departments, he knew about the forthcoming Turbo model. By 1976, well before the production car was ready for sale, the competitions department had begun work on an ultra-powerful turbo of their own.

Rally engineer Borje Jarl talked to me in Sweden recently, and gave me a fascinating insight into the

work which was done 'In no more than three or four weeks, Sodertaljc produced a modified Turbo engine, with a 6.5:1 compression ratio, and a bigger turbine; with a standard camshaft this gave only 180 bhp, but when we tested against a 230 bhp 16-valve car on our special track we found that the Turbo car was faster. The torque was 32 mkg (231 lb.ft.) and that counted—the car was very easy to drive.

'Further development of the 16-valve engine had been to raise the size of the engine to 2.2-litres [with a 95 mm bore—AAGR], but this was expensive and

A strong team in every sense. That legend of rallying, Erik Carlsson, between Stig Blomqvist (his right) and Per Eklund, in 1975, with 'works' Saab V4 and 99 EMS Rally cars also in shot. The 99 Turbo was going to make Saab even more competitive

A 1980 'works' rally car,
showing entirely different
manifolding from the
production car. All this
helped raise power to more
than 270 bhp on some engines

difficult, so we decided to concentrate on the Turbo.

'We were told that with this engine we could get 350 bhp, no problem, but that would make the car very difficult to drive the car, the same as with the 16 valve engine. So, all the time we were looking for low-level horsepower and torque—to do this, we worked through *all* the Garrett turbochargers, and there were many at this stage!

'But all the time we were looking for power all the time, right through the rev range. By reducing the compression ratio, we arranged that the base engine, really without the turbo working, was never in use. By the end we could get up to 300 bhp in the rally car, and it was still very easy to drive. On camshafts, our first step was to go from the Turbo to the EMS (injection) profile, then we tried to raise the lift as much as possible. We got *so much* power, you know, that we kept down to a 6.5:1 compression ratio, but we could still have gone back to 7.2:1, the standard compression ratio, if necessary.'

Borje Jarl's comments on rev limits were even more illuminating 'The drivers *could* use 9000 rpm

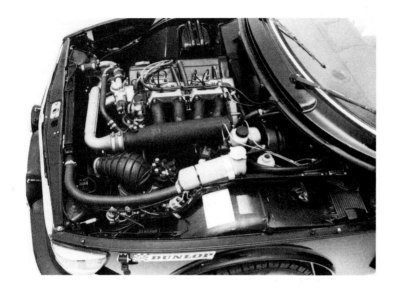

*The 'inlet' side of the 1980 99
Turbo 'works' rally car*

for the 16-valve or the Turbo—after which the
connecting rods and the pistons would begin to give
trouble. In practice, with the Turbos they used 7500
rpm in the intermediate gears (with the 16-valve
they had to use 8500/9000 rpm to keep the car
going)—and in top gear they used whatever was
available. But above 7500 the torque was dropping
away fast.

'We used special four-speed gearboxes throughout, but now there is also a rally version of the five-
speed box as well, but it has never been used in
competition.

'The maximum boost we ever used on rally
engines was 1.7 Bar [which is more than 24 psi], but
there was more to come. . . .'

Power, therefore, was never going to be a problem
with a 'works' Turbo in rallying, nor apparently
were problems of driveability ever going to require
particular genius from the drivers. The exigencies
of homologation, however, meant that the car
would have to be based on the standard three-door
EMS/Turbo bodyshell. Not only was this signi-

Right *The fascia of a 'works' 99 Turbo in 1980, featuring two-way radio for the co-driver to use, and extra electrical fuses and relays ahead of the co-driver's seat. The boost gauge was special, and you may be sure that Stig Blomqvist ignored the 6000 rpm 'limit' still marked on the rev-counter!*

Below *There's evidence here. Blomqvist and Cederserg winning the 1980 South Swedish Rally*

ficantly heavier than the more basic two-door saloon style (the penalty was about 40 kg/88 lb), but the car itself was inherently very solid in any case. Figures published in the *World Rallying* annual for 1979 suggest that the rallying Turbo was at least 120 kg/265 lb heavier than the World Championship winning Ford Escort RS, and that the peak power output was about the same.

Problems with the rallying Turbo were all connected with the power being unleashed from the engine. The standard exhaust manifolds, for instance, would quite literally begin to melt at the temperatures the 250 bhp 'stage 1' rally engine produced (just a glance at the red-heat condition manifolds exhibit in test bed conditions proves that), while similar heat build-up conditions led to a wholesale re-design of the inlet manifolds too.

Consider, for a moment, the demands put on the transmission, and those which also fell upon the braking system. There was so much torque on the developed rally engine (34 mkg/246 lb ft even in 1978, when power tuning was in its infancy) that the gearbox, final drive, and drive shafts all had an extremely hard time. Fortunately, extensive development had already taken place for the 16-valve cars, and the latest special components could all be expected to stand up to the job. Even though a free-wheel was not fitted to the transmission (that famous Saab front-wheel-drive feature had been discontinued) the Swedish drivers' skilful use of left-foot-braking to balance the car for hard cornering make the brakes work enormously hard. In the stress of battle, therefore, it was nothing to see the front brake discs glowing red at the end of a stage, then to see the bonnet raised and the exhaust manifold doing its best to match the colour. It was no wonder that the single biggest problem with the Turbo was heat, and the insulation of various components from its effects took time to develop.

Indeed, Saab's enthusiast team began to realize how lucky they had always been with previous cars, which had not really needed too much modification to make them competitive; the Turbo was a veritable Supercar from the day it was completed, and the spectators looked forward avidly to seeing it in action.

One tiny point illustrates the new problems to be faced—compared with any Saab rally car of the last 10 years or so, the Turbo was much quieter, for turbochargers tend to 'eat' the inherent noise leaving the engine through the exhaust manifold. The faster the car went on a stage, the quieter it seemed to become, and extra loud horns had to be fitted to warn wandering spectators of its approach!

The 'works' Turbo was not ready for competition at the beginning of 1978, which explains why long-time team driver Stig Blomqvist used a mid-engined Lancia Stratos to finish fourth overall in February's Swedish Rally. Development during the year was somewhat protracted, though Blomqvist first used the car in the British TV Rallysprint at Esgair Dafydd, finishing fourth overall behind an Escort RS, a TR7 V8 and another Escort.

The appearance of two three-door 'works' Turbos on the Lombard-RAC Rally of 1978 was really the start of a more concentrated programme, when Blomqvist and Per Eklund started in two Group 2 cars. They were certainly fast, and looked impressive in Polar Caravans' sponsorship colours, but both destroyed their transmissions before half distance.

In 1979, Bo Hellberg and his young assistant Bo Swaner took advantage of the widening of the Turbo production-car range, for not only did they manage to fit power-assisted steering to the rally cars (the steering, with fat tyres and more than 250 bhp to be harnessed, could be very heavy in normal manual trim), but they completed a very complex

process of homologation for their cars. The three-door had been approved as a Group 4 car in January 1978; it had been upgraded to Group 1 in October (Group 1 regulations require 5000 examples of the basic model to be built in a 12-month period, and Saab had no difficulty in satisfying this requirement). In February 1979 they also homologated the lighter two-door Turbo saloon into Group 4 (400-off production needed), but they had this upgraded to Group 2 (1000 produced) just one month later. Although it was not important to them at this stage, they also had the larger 900 Turbo approved in Group 2 as well.

The season could not possibly have started better for the factory, for Stig Blomqvist entered and won the Swedish Rally in a two-door Turbo during

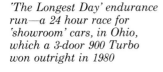

'The Longest Day' endurance run—a 24 hour race for 'showroom' cars, in Ohio, which a 3-door 900 Turbo won outright in 1980

February, while one week later he drove another Turbo (this time a three-door, which was therefore slightly heavier) to win the British Mintex International event. Victory in the Swedish was particularly sweet, not only because it was 'at home', and because it was the first for the Saab Turbo, but also because it was the first-ever World Championship victory for a turbocharged car.

The rest of the season, however, was something of an anti-climax. Not that the cars and drivers were not competitive; they had such a limited programme. No further World Championship points were scored, amazingly because cars were not even entered in the Finnish Rally of 1000 Lakes, while both the drivers who started the Lombard-RAC Rally had accidents; the reason for Stig Blomqvist's

In Britain, some raced and rallycrossed their Turbos with success, some with rather less success . . .

retirement was officially given as 'blown engine' at one stage, but this actually happened when he was trying to extract the car from its final resting place!

In the British Open series, Stig used a two-door in the newly-formed Dealer Team entry, and managed to take sixth place on the Circuit of Ireland, eighth on the Welsh, and seventh on the Scottish, while he also won the South Swedish event, which was a qualifying round for the European Championship. But in spite of the fact that his car was producing 275 bhp by the end of the season—more than any other top-class contender—it was proving more and more difficult for a Superstar like Blomqvist to win in a car not ideally suited to the task.

In 1980 Blomqvist and Saab tried again. Their Saab Dealer Team season in the UK was even more frustrating than before, for breakage after breakage intervened, and the usually consistent Blomqvist also found time to have a shunt, which was not at all like him. In their review of the British season, *Autosport* said that 'After Saab successes of the past, 1980 will go down as a year they would prefer to forget.'

For the first time in years, Saab failed to win a single World Championship point in the Makes contest, although Stig Blomqvist took second place on the Swedish (behind Anders Kullang's Opel Ascona 400), which only counted towards the Drivers' crown. But once again there were no entries in the 1000 Lakes, and Blomqvist's successes were confined to outright victories in the Boucles de Spa and South Sweden, with second place (to Darniche's Lancia Stratos) in the Costa Smeralda event.

The problem, seemingly insoluble for Saab, as it was for other experienced manufacturers, was that the Turbo had come up against the front-wheel-drive barrier—the point at which extra power fed through the front wheels of a rally car (which also have to be steered and braked) can almost be counter-productive. It was not that Blomqvist was losing his touch (wonderful performances behind the wheel of a four-wheel-drive Audi Quattro in 1982 certainly disproved that one), nor was it that the Turbo rally car was not fast enough in a straight line—it was merely that it could not be urged around corners, or achieve enough traction out of them, as well as more conventional rear-drive machines like the Opels, Vauxhalls, Fords and Fiats.

Saab, in any case, could see that things were going to get worse for them, rather than better, not only because a new set of Group A and Group B rules were due to be enforced from 1 January 1982, but because they could see 'specials' like the mid-engined Renault 5 Turbo and the fabulous four-wheel-drive Audi Quattro coming along as well. It was with a heavy heart, though with a great deal of pride, therefore, that they withdrew from International motor sport at the end of 1980. For the first time since the early 1950s, no more 'works' Saabs would be seen in the forests, or on the snow-bound tracks of the world.

In the meantime, Saab had also become interested in the rally cross business, not only because their cars were very suitable for the rough-and-tumble of this sport, but because there was also quite a lot of TV exposure, particularly for successful competitions! The precedents were excellent, for the original turbocharged 96 V4 of 1972 had become competitive by 1976; thus when Blomqvist began to use a 290 bhp rally cross two-door Turbo in 1979, he was always likely to be a winner.

Although Saab 99s had been raced in the United States since the mid 1970s (with American PR manager Len Lonnegran becoming competitions manager, and a team of three cars to look after), the Turbo did not come on the scene until 1979, when it became eligible for Showroom Stock Class A and B categories. This was a challenging series, for it also included cars like the Porsche 924 and the Datsun 280Z coupés, which might have been 'showroom', but were also given under-the-counter support by their parent factories.

The end of season results, however, tell their own story, with Saab winning the Class A *and* Class B categories outright. In 1980 they went further, when a three-door 900 Turbo driven by four heros (including two *Road & Track* journalists) won the 'Longest Day' 24-hour Showroom in Ohio.

There was, it seemed, no limit to the versatility of the Turbo—but then that, after all, is what well-designed turbocharged engines are all about. In the 1980s, I am sure, we will hear much more about this engine, and what it can achieve.

Specifications

Note All Saab 99s and Saab 900s, of whatever engine size, tune, or styling derivation, have been developed from the same basic 'chassis', structure, and mechanical layout. All Saab 99s have been built on the same 97.5 in. wheelbase, while the Saab 900 was launched with a 99.4 in. wheelbase, the increase being effectively provided ahead of the driver's toeboard.

On the 99 range, two-door, three-door, four-door and five-door versions were all built from time to time, while on the 900 range there have been three-door, four-door and five-door derivatives.

99 Turbo

General layout Series-production car, built in various types on same underpan, as two-door saloon, or as three-door or five-door Combi coupé, with large hatchback. Pressed-steel unit construction body/chassis unit without separate chassis. Front engine, and front wheel drive, with independent front suspension, rack and pinion steering, and 'dead' rear axle layout. No estate car, or open derivatives.

Normal 'non-USA' specification

Engine Type Four cylinders, in line, with single overhead camshaft cylinder head, in line valves. Cylinder block fore-and-aft in car, inclined at 45 degrees to vertical as installed in the car.
Bore, stroke and capacity 90.0×78.0 mm$=1985$ cc (3.54×3.07 in.$=121.0$ cu. in.)
Compression ratio (nominal) 7.2:1.
Cylinder head Aluminium alloy, with cross-flow breathing and individual inlet and exhaust ports. Two valves per cylinder, in line, and vertically aligned with axis of cylinder bore. Combustion chambers partly in head, and partly in crown of pistons. Single camshaft mounted in cylinder head, operating valves via inverted 'bucket' tappets, and driven from end of crankshaft by duplex chain.
Cylinder block Combined with crankcase, in cast iron, with no cylinder liners, and with five crankshaft main bearings.
Crankshaft In forged steel, counterweighted, fully balanced, and carried in five main bearings.

Pistons Light alloy.

Carburation Bosch K-Jetronic indirect fuel injection, plus Garrett AiResearch turbocharger, delivering air at maximum 10 PSI boost. Turbocharger at right front corner of front-mounted engine.

Power output 145 bhp (DIN) at 5000 rpm; maximum torque 174 lb ft at 3000 rpm.

Transmission Type Front-wheel-drive layout, all in unit with front-mounted engine. Engine drives forward through single-plate clutch, then by Morse chain to all-synchromesh gearbox ahead of/under the engine, and direct to final-drive unit under the engine, then driving front wheels by universally jointed, exposed, drive shafts.

Gearbox Four-speed, all-synchromesh, manual gearbox, driven from clutch output shaft by Morse chain. With remote control selection, and centre gear change.

Internal gear ratios Primary chain reduction 0.9:1. Gears, 3.693, 2.194, 1.472, 1.00, reverse 4.002:1.

Final drive, and ratio Spiral bevel gears, 3.89:1.

Chassis and suspension Type Pressed-steel unit-construction bodyshell in a variety of types all on same basic underpan, inner and structural panels; available during life of car in two-door saloon (with normal separate boot), three-door and five-door Combi (USA=Wagonback) models with hatchback. All structural stress-carrying members built into bodyshell.

Front suspension Independent, by coil springs and wishbones, with telescopic dampers. No anti-roll bar.

Steering Rack and pinion, 4.1 turns lock-to-lock.

Rear suspension By 'dead' axle beam, coil springs, leading and trailing radius arms forming Watts linkages, and Panhard rod, with telescopic dampers. No anti-roll bar.

Wheels and tyres Cast light-alloy disc wheels, with four-stud bolt-on fixings. 15 in. diameter rims, and 5.5 in. rim width. 175/70-15 in. radial ply tyres.

Brakes ATE disc brakes for all four wheels, hydraulically operated through divided hydraulic circuits, with vacuum servo assistance. 11.0 in. front discs, 10.6 in. rear discs. Handbrake operating separately on front wheels, lever centrally mounted, between seats.

Bodywork All cars built as full five-seaters. Two-door saloons with normal separate boot and conventional lid. Three-door and five-door Combi coupés with two or four passenger doors and with full-depth hatchback incorporating

aerodynamic spoiler beneath bottom of rear window glass. All cars with conventional steel panels.
Major dimensions Wheelbase 8 ft 1.5 in. (247.7 cm) Track, front 4 ft 7.1 in. (140 cm) Track, rear 4 ft 7.9 in. (142 cm) Overall length (2-door) 14 ft 6 in. (442 cm) Overall length (3-door and 5-door) 14 ft 10.3 in. (453 cm) Overall width 5 ft 6.5 in. (169 cm) Overall height 4 ft 8.5 in. (143.5 cm) Turning circle 34 ft 6 in. (10.5 m) Kerb weight (approx.) (2-door) 2491 lb (1130 kg), (3-door) 2700 lb (1224 kg), (5-door) 2720 lb (1233 kg).

USA Specification

The USA-model 99 Turbo was basically the same as that sold in Europe, except for the following technical differences:
Engine power outputs 137 bhp (DIN) at 5000 rpm; maximum torque 160 lb ft at 3500 rpm.
Turbocharging Maximum boost 7 PSI.

Development changes

1979 models Ratio of primary reduction chain drive changed to 0.839:1.
1980 models Optional 5-speed all-synchromesh gearbox made available. Primary reduction chain drive ratio 0.781:1. Gear ratios 4.25, 2.562, 1.72, 1.236, 1.000, reverse 4.675:1.
1981 models Turbocharged 99 now discontinued, in favour of turbocharged 900.

900 Turbo

General layout 900 was reworked derivative of 99 model, with same basic centre sections, passenger cabins and tails as equivalent 99s, but new longer wheelbase, and front end structure and sheet metal. As before, front engine with front wheel drive. No estate car, or open derivatives.

Technical specification of normal 'non-USA' models as for 99 Turbos, except for:

Transmission European versions as for 99, but USA versions with different primary reduction chain drive gearing.
Steering Rack and pinion, with 3.7 turns lock-to-lock, and power assistance.
Wheels and tyres 3-door 195/60HR-15 in. Pirelli P6 radial ply tyres, on 6.0 in. rim width wheels. 5-door 180/65HR-390 mm Michelin TRX radial-ply tyres on 150 mm rim width wheels.
Bodywork Two-door conventional saloons not available. Original range comprised three-door and five-door models.
Major dimensions Wheelbase 8 ft 3.4 in. (252.5 cm) Track, front 4 ft 7.9 in. (142 cm) Track, rear 4 ft 8.3 in. (143 cm) Overall length 15 ft 6.5 in. (474 cm) Overall width 5 ft 6.5 in. (169 cm) Overall height 4 ft 8.25 in. (142 cm) Turning circle

37 ft 0 in. (11.3 m) Kerb weight (approx.) (3-door) 2650 lb (1202 kg) (5-door) 2650 lb (1202 kg).

USA Specification

The USA-model 900 Turbo was basically the same as that sold in Europe, except for the following technical differences:
Engine power outputs 137 bhp (DIN) at 5000 rpm; maximum torque 160 lb ft at 3500 rpm.
Transmission Same gear ratios, but 0.9:1 primary reduction chain drive gearing.

Development changes

1980 models Optional 5-speed all-synchromesh gearbox made available. Primary reduction chain drive ratio 0.781:1. Gear ratios 4.25, 2.562, 1.719, 1.236, 1.000, reverse 4.675:1.
1981 models Four-door 'booted' saloon added to range. Both types of manual gearbox given lower (higher numerical ratio) bottom gears. New ratio sets: 4-speed: 3.882, 2.194, 1.473, 1.000, reverse 4.271:1. 5-speed: 4.533, 2.562, 1.719, 1.236, 1.000, reverse 4.987:1.
Borg-Warner 3-speed automatic transmission became available on 4-door and 5-door models. Ratios as follows: Primary reduction chain drive 0.968:1. Internal gear ratios: 2.39, 1.45, 1.000, reverse 2.09:1.
1982 models APC engine monitoring equipment for some markets. Final drive ratio raised to 3.667:1 and primary chain ratios modified to suit: 4-speed gearbox: Primary chain ratio 0.9:1. 5-speed gearbox: Primary chain ratio 0.839:1.
1983 models APC engine controls for all markets. Launch of long-wheelbase 900 Turbo CD—like 4-door 900 Turbo, but with wheelbase increased to 8 ft 11.3 in. (272.5 cm) to increase space for rear seat passengers; overall length increased to 16 ft 2.5 in. (494 cm). Automatic transmission standard. Unladen weight 2722 lb (1234 kg).

Turbo production figures: 1977 to 1982

Production of Saab Turbos began in 1977, the 99 Turbo having been launched at the Frankfurt Motor Show in September of that year. The 900 Turbo was launched in May 1978. Production of 99 Turbos ended in 1980 (though the cars were still listed into 1981).

Calendar year production

Year	99 Turbo	900 Turbo	Total 99 production	Total 900 production
1977	1066	—	60,316	—
1978	6672	3814	45,851	17,244
1979	1506	10,700	22,443	52,478
1980	1363	15,189	17,108	48,646
1981	—	19,424	13,381	58,011
1982	—	20,346	20,006	63,551
Running totals	10,607	69,473	179,105	234,930

Model year production

Like nearly every one of the world's car manufacturers, Saab regulate their production on a 'model year' rather than a 'calendar year' basis. This means that 'model year' production begins immediately after the summer holiday, and ends immediately before the next. According to motor industry convention, production of 1983 'model year' cars began in August 1982, and ended in July 1983.

This might sound crazy, but one very good reason justifying it is that there is a lengthy 'pipeline' effect from Sweden to North America, and an early start to the 'year' means that deliveries in the USA can begin as soon as the cars arrive.

On this basis, 'model year' production of Saab Turbos has been as follows:

Model year	99 Turbo	900 Turbo
1977	100	—
1978	6376	—
1979	1798	8947
1980	2333	14,535
1981	—	14,844
1982	—	19,851
1983	—	12,922 (*up to the end of Jan. 1983*)
Running totals	10,607	71,099

Saab Turbo deliveries—by country—to the end of 1982

As might be expected, the Turbo has been most popular in the United States in the first five years of its career. However, it has sold very well in Europe, and other countries, as these two 'league tables' show

99 Turbo deliveries		900 Turbo deliveries	
USA	4233	USA	24,334
Great Britain	2027	Sweden	9487
Sweden	1570	Great Britain	5486
West Germany	1039	Italy	4920
Switzerland	911	West Germany	4163
Holland	668	Tax Free Sales	2769
Finland	203	Switzerland	1933
Canada	180	Holland	1164
Tax Free Sales	163	Belgium	1106
Belgium	113	Finland	734
Austria	84	Australia	655
France	51	France	655
Norway	46	Portugal and Spain	589
Eastern Europe	30	Austria	570
Italy	27	Canada	492
Denmark	27	Denmark	461
Republic of Ireland	17	Japan	459
Australia	11	Norway	306
		Republic of Ireland	296
		South American continent	124

—a surprisingly high number have been sold to South America, and to Japan, both notoriously 'difficult' for car makers from less obviously 'neutral' countries to penetrate. At the time of writing, therefore, something like 36 per cent of all Saab Turbos have been delivered to the USA.

Acknowledgements

I ought to start by thanking Erik Carlsson for introducing me to Saab motoring, to Harry Webster of Standard-Triumph for ensuring that I was in the right place at the right time, and to my friends at *Autocar* for enabling me to make close contact with Saab engineeres over the years. For arranging my trip to Trollhättan, my thanks go to John Edwards and Ian Adcock of Saab (GB), and to Peter Salzer of Saab-Scania. I'm indebted to Per Gillbrand, Nils-Gunnar Svensson, Neils-Uno Hakansson and Borje Jarl, for helping me with the information, and the detailed research. It was also splendid to get a real taste of the true 'Saab spirit'. Many people helped photographer Mirco Decet put this book together from an illustrative point of view. We must thank the following: Gerald Foster who photographed cars at Star Lincoln Mercury Saab in Glendale, CA.; Norman James at what was Triumph cars in Coventry, Peter Bull at Haymill Motors Ltd, Farnham Common; Dermot Bambridge at Scania (GB) Ltd in Milton Keynes; Jerry Sloniger; Studio Oy of Helsinki; Per Lidstrom of Uppsala in Sweden; Bob Fischer of St Louis and Lat. Finally there were the several Saab organizations; Peter Salzer co-ordinating the efforts of Nykoping and Linkoping, Len Lonnegren of Saab-Scania of America Inc. in Orange, Conn., and the PR department at Saab (GB) Ltd in Marlow.

Index